wot T

D0550405

Gardening with
Hebes

700022732601

Gardening with Hebes

CHRIS & VALERIE WHEELER

GUILD OF MASTER CRAFTSMAN PUBLICATIONS

WORCESTERSHIRE COUNTY COUNCIL	
260	
Cypher	09.09.02
635.976	£12.95

First published 2002 by

Guild of Master Craftsman Publications Ltd

Castle Place, 166 High Street,

Lewes, East Sussex BN7 1XU

Text © Chris and Valerie Wheeler 2002

© in the work GMC Publications 2002

Photographs © Chris Wheeler 2002

Drawings © Melanie Clitheroe 2002

ISBN 1 86108 291 6

All rights reserved

The right of Chris and Valerie Wheeler to be identified as the
authors of this work has been asserted in accordance with the
Copyright Designs and Patents Act 1988, sections 77 and 78.

No part of this publication may be reproduced, stored in a
retrieval system or transmitted in any form or by any means
without the prior permission of the publisher and copyright
owner.

The publishers and authors can accept no legal responsibility
for any consequences arising from the application of
information, advice or instructions given in this publication.

A catalogue record for this book is available from the British
Library.

Edited by Stephen Haynes

Book and cover designed by Fineline Studios

Set in Minion

Colour origination by Viscan Graphics (Singapore)

Printed in China by Sun Fung Offset Binding Co Ltd

Acknowledgements

We are grateful to the following for allowing us
to photograph their gardens: Cliff and Pat Jarrett;
John and Betty Wheeler; John and Lucy Fox.
Also to Anne Tweddle for information on her
homeland, New Zealand.

Contents

Introduction

This book combines ideas on how to enhance your garden with hebes and thorough practical advice on growing and maintaining them. The popularity and appeal of these attractive shrubs has been steadily increasing during the last 20 to 30 years, matched by a renewed interest in breeding and a large number of new introductions.

Hebes are a diverse group of plants, suitable for growing in one way or another in just about every garden. The range includes tiny species suitable for sink gardens, dwarf hummocks for rock gardens, bushy shrubs, ground-cover types, and large, spectacular flowering varieties for the border. Many are reliable, easy shrubs to grow, rewarding us with long flowering displays and valuable evergreen foliage, while others provide interesting foliage or good winter leaf colours. There are also choice, unusual species that can be a challenge to grow.

This book aims to show you how to enliven your garden by planting hebes in a wide variety of ways, incorporating them into borders, raised beds, sinks and containers, and utilizing them for ground cover and edging. It also demonstrates innovative ways of using them as hedges and training them as standards and topiary.

There is a general misconception that hebes are not hardy, and while this is true of some, it is definitely not the case for the majority. We hope this book will help to change this view, showing that a vast number of hebes are hardy given the correct growing conditions: an open, sunny position in well-drained soil that does not dry out.

Clear practical advice, from the authors' own long experience, is supported by step-by-step photographs of cultivation techniques. The diversity of hebe foliage and flower, and their versatility in the garden, are illustrated in the numerous colour photographs throughout the book.

We hope gardeners of all abilities will be inspired to consider planting more hebes, searching out both well-known and more unusual varieties. By encouraging different ways of growing them, we hope to increase the knowledge and wider use of this wonderful group of plants, which can provide so much interest and colour in gardens of any size or scale.

Hebe 'Nicola's Blush'

CHAPTER 1

Origins and characteristics

The hebe's native homeland

New Zealand is the home of a huge variety of plants that are rarely found elsewhere. This phenomenon is largely due to the isolation of the two islands that comprise New Zealand. The genus *Hebe* is found throughout New Zealand, on both North and South Islands, and makes up the largest genus of plants there. However, not many species occur on both islands, and there is huge variation within the genus, which is not surprising considering the enormous variation in both climate and terrain throughout the islands. In fact, some species are found only in particular locations, which demonstrates just how unique this country is in terms of its plants.

Although the majority of hebes originate from New Zealand, a few are found in Tasmania, Australia, South America and the Falkland Islands.

Habitat and climate

The types of habitat found in New Zealand are extremely varied. There are coastal cliffs, with their high winds and salt spray; mountains, which extend much of the length of the country, giving

areas above the snowline as well as lower down; moist, peaty areas around the lakes; wet rainforests; near-desert regions; and cold inland areas. As both islands are long and slender in shape, there is a very long coastline and no part is really very far from the coast.

The climate shows similar variation. Extremely dry regions contrast with very wet areas; the average rainfall is high for the whole of New Zealand, but some parts experience particularly high rainfall. There are frequently very strong winds. Some parts have mild winters and hardly any frosts, while others often suffer both snow and frost.

It follows that the variation among species in the genus *Hebe* is enormous, as they can be found in so many different types of habitat with such a wide variation in climate. Those that originate from coastal regions are better able to tolerate salt spray, which is why these grow so well in coastal areas elsewhere. They are also adapted to withstand the strong winds prevalent in these regions. Hebes that grow in mountainous areas, with their extreme changes in temperature, are tough, hardy and more compact, with thick, leathery leaves to withstand both hot, dry spells and cold winds and intermittent snow.

Hebe 'Heidi'

Why hebes are suited to northern climates

The variation in climate that hebes experience in their native land means that some species are totally hardy in the more northerly countries (such as Britain), while others are more tender and will not survive a cold northern winter. Climate varies considerably between the two islands, with South Island having the more temperate climate. The inland areas of South Island tend to be cold, with frost and snow over winter, so species from here are hardier in cold weather than those from the northern end of North Island, which has a more subtropical climate, with very little frost.

Hebes from the temperate South Island are ideal for growing in cooler parts of the world, and many species are reliably hardy, whereas those originating in North Island are likely to be more tender. Some newer hebes have been bred specifically for hardiness among other desirable traits – for example, the 'Wiri' series bred at Auckland Botanic Gardens.

Many hebes have already been in cultivation for a long time. *Hebe* 'Fairfieldii' was discovered at the end of the nineteenth century, for instance, and both *H.* 'Autumn Glory' and *H.* 'Edinensis' were raised at the beginning of the twentieth century.

Hebes have become extremely popular and many new hybrids have been introduced and named since the 1970s, when there was a resurgence of interest. In the UK, Graham Hutchins from Essex has contributed many new hebes, both from the wild in New Zealand and by breeding. In New Zealand, Jack Hobbs of Auckland Botanic Gardens has done much work on hybridizing hebes, resulting in several floriferous, attractive and disease-free forms being released in the 1980s.

Breeding of hebes

Hebes are capable of hybridizing, or crossing with each other, very freely. In the wild, hebes show great variation even within their own species: there may be differences in their leaves or flowers, or they may grow in a different type of habitat. When different species occur within close proximity to each other, even more variety can occur as one species hybridizes with another.

The same thing readily happens in cultivation, with hebes hybridizing in the garden. You can often find young seedlings appearing under or around mature plants, and these may well be the result of crosses between different plants. It is important not to assume that any seedlings are the same as the plant they are found adjacent to: this has been the cause of endless confusion in the nursery trade, causing difficulties in the correct naming and identification of hebes. If seedlings are sold under their presumed parents' name, different plants are going to be propagated and distributed with the same name. These plants may be similar, but will not be identical; they may even be completely different. Hebes should always be propagated vegetatively (that is, from cuttings), in order to maintain their correct form.

Hebe seedlings have also been passed around with completely made-up names – perhaps the donor's name – which causes further confusion. If you do grow on or pass around any seedling-grown plants, make sure they are labelled as such.

There are International Codes for the nomenclature of plants and cultivated plants, which are too detailed for this book to delve into.

Veronica austriaca 'Ionian Skies'

Hebe characteristics

What is a hebe?

Hebes are ornamental evergreen shrubs, belonging to the family *Scrophulariaceae,* and there are about one hundred species. They are named in honour of Hebe, the Greek goddess of youth who was cupbearer to the gods.

All hebes were formerly included under the genus *Veronica,* which also used to contain *Parahebe;* these were later split up into three distinct genera, with the new genus *Hebe* being formed around 1926. In older books and journals, you will find information and research on hebes under their previous names.

Veronica is still a very large genus, now restricted to herbaceous species from northern temperate regions, and the species usually have blue flowers in racemes. Members of the genus *Hebe* (often still known as 'shrubby veronicas') are evergreen, with a woody or shrubby growth habit, and comprise those species from the southern hemisphere. *Parahebe* is a small genus of semi-woody evergreen shrubs, mainly from New Zealand, which are

Parahebe catarractae 'Delight'

summer-flowering, bearing loose racemes of flowers in white or shades of blue or pink. There are also differences in the division of seed in the seed capsules, and differences in chromosome numbers, between these last two genera.

Hebes are spring- to autumn-flowering shrubs, and the majority of wild species have white flowers, as do most New Zealand plants. Flowers consist of simple or branched racemes, spikes or panicles, each bearing several small flowers. In the majority of cases, these arise from the leaf axil (the place where the leaf joins the stem), but in others they are borne at the end of a shoot. Cultivated varieties can have flowers of white, pink or shades of lilac, mauve and purple. Flower buds are sometimes a deeper shade than the open flower, and flowers often fade as they age, giving a two-tone effect that can be very attractive.

Characteristic features of hebes

Here we have set out, with explanations of botanical terms where necessary, those features that distinguish hebes, together with the variations within them.

Leaves

The leaves are held in opposite pairs along the stems. They are evergreen, with great variation in size. To give you some indication, the leaves of *Hebe buchananii* 'Minor' are about 4 × 2mm (⅛ × 1/16in), those of *H.* 'Nicola's Blush' 40 × 13mm (1½ × ½in), and those of *H. salicifolia* 110 × 22mm (4¼ × ⅞in). They may be flat, concave or convex, with a surface that is matt or glossy. The leaf itself can be relatively thin, or thick and somewhat fleshy, or leathery in texture. The leaf margins are often smooth, but can have a few notches or be toothed all round. Colours include

Small, grey-green, tightly packed leaves of *Hebe topiaria*

The large, glossy, purple-flushed leaves of *Hebe* 'Amy'

all shades of green, from deep green to bright, fresh green and light green; yellow-green; olive; old gold; golden; silvery-blue, grey-blue and grey-green. Many are flushed or margined with purple or red. Some have variegated leaves, sometimes made even more colourful by being suffused with deeper colours. The midrib, or main central vein of the leaf, may be coloured differently from the leaf itself.

The leaves of some hebes, notably the appropriately named whipcords and their hybrids, are pressed closely or flatly against the stem; these are referred to as being **adpressed**.

Whipcord hebes, which vaguely resemble conifers and are often mistaken for such, are a distinctive group, with both juvenile and adult foliage. Juvenile leaves are usually soft and feathery, spreading out from the branch, whereas adult foliage is small, overlapping and tightly pressed to the stems, producing the characteristic 'whipcord' effect. This tight leaf growth minimizes transpiration in the strong winds of their natural habitat. These plants tend to be relatively slow-growing, and they provide interesting foliage contrasts for the garden.

Stems

Some hebes have slender, quite whippy stems, while others are thicker or even quite stout. The surface may be smooth or roughly textured, and is usually coloured brown or grey when older. Young stems are often coloured green, yellow-green or purple.

The soft, feathery, juvenile foliage of *Hebe cupressoides* 'Boughton Dome'

The distinctive, cord-like branches of the whipcord *Hebe hectorii*

Elegant, tapering raceme of *Hebe* 'Bowles's Hybrid'

Flowers

The flowers of hebes show considerable variety in form, size and density, though all have a structure that falls into the following categories:

- A **spike** is a simple elongated inflorescence in which the individual flowers have no stalk (that is, they are **sessile**). Each flower sits directly on the flower stem. Spikes may be short or long, slender and tapering, or stubby, with individual flowers densely packed together or spaced further apart.
- A **raceme** differs in that each individual flower has its own stem along the main flowering stem. Again, the appearance of a raceme depends on the spacing and number of these flowers, and can be short, dense and compact, or longer, more slender and graceful. Flowers can be closely packed together or more open, giving a looser structure.

Dense, clustered racemes of *Hebe decumbens*

Panicle of *Hebe hulkeana*

Terminal raceme of *Hebe* 'Baby Marie'

◆ Some hebes have **panicles** of flowers, which are in effect branched racemes. Individual flowers are on stalks along flowering stems, which branch out from a main flowering stem. These give a very airy effect.

Each of these structures may be lateral or terminal.

◆ A **lateral** raceme, for example, is borne on the side of a stem, arising from a leaf axil. The majority of hebes have lateral flowers.

◆ A **terminal** panicle, for example, is borne at the very end of a branch, right at the tip.

Flowers are generally smaller and more subtle in both appearance and colour in dwarf hebes, particularly species plants (that is, natural rather than cultivated ones), than in the larger hybrid hebes with their long, flamboyant flowers. In recent years, however, new dwarf varieties have been bred with deeper-coloured flowers in shades of pink and purple.

The timing and frequency of flowering varies considerably. Some hebes regularly flower at one particular time of year only, and have a mass of bloom all at once. Others are more sporadic or fleeting, while some produce flowers twice in a year, or a succession of flowers over many weeks or months. With a careful selection of plants, it is possible to have some in flower for much of the year.

Growth habits

Hebes vary enormously in the way that they grow, which adds to their great versatility in the garden. Different species or varieties may be prostrate, decumbent, spreading, bushy, or upright. In addition, the individual plant may be compact or more open-branched, densely covered in foliage or clothed more sparsely in leaves, revealing more of the stem.

Let's take a look at the main shapes and growth habits of hebes. Most hebes fall into one or other of the following categories. We describe some examples of each, to demonstrate the variety within each category.

Prostrate hebes produce branches that grow horizontally, lying flat or very close to the ground. *H. chathamica* has very closely overlapping stems, growing right down at ground level and forming a low mound, well clothed in neat leaves. *H.* 'County Park' has masses of small leaves clothing its

horizontal stems, while *H. albicans* 'Sussex Carpet' has more widely spaced leaves on long branches, which overlap each other, gradually producing a very low, tiered effect. Some hebes, such as *H.* 'Dazzler', are **semi-prostrate**, their stems horizontal but the plant growing taller.

In some hebes, the branches grow horizontally, lying along the ground or close to it, but the tips of the shoots then turn upwards, or ascend. These **decumbent** forms include *H.* 'Wingletye' with glaucous foliage and *H.* 'Youngii', a smaller form with green leaves. *H. decumbens*, with its literal species name, is a most attractive hebe with shiny green leaves on dark stems. The habit of these hebes makes the fresh new growth at the tips easily visible.

Spreading or **arching** hebes can grow into wide bushes, the branches growing out at an angle; some form a kind of vase-shape, lower in the centre, with the branches growing outwards and upwards. *H. pimeleoides* 'Quicksilver' has slender, open branches spreading widely, somewhat arching, with very small, widely spaced leaves. *H. ochracea* 'James Stirling' is completely different, forming a dense, flat-topped vase shape, its stout branches covered in tiny scale-like leaves.

There is a huge range of **bushy** hebes, in which a rounded, bushy shape is produced by means of the branches growing out from the main upright stems. These hebes can be tight and compact, with short, many-branched stems packed close together, forming a neat bun shape, or more open, with longer branches spaced further apart. Bushes may be as wide or wider than their height. *H. topiaria* has a neat, clipped appearance, with dense stems covered in small leaves; *H. raoulii* var. *maccaskillii* is a tiny, bushy species with very slender stems; *H. albicans* is a rounded bush well clothed in foliage on much-branched stems; *H.* 'Nicola's Blush' is wider than it is

Hebe topiaria has a naturally trim, tidy shape

The bushy, layered effect of *Hebe* 'Wiri Mist'

high, with more open stems and larger leaves, forming a looser, rounded shape. Many of the larger hebes are also bushy in outline.

Other hebes are **erect**, with stems and branches growing upright. They are often more sparsely branched than the others, and usually taller than they are high, whether they are dwarf or larger hebes. *H. raoulii* var. *pentasepala* is a distinctive upright, albeit tiny, species, while *H. pauciramosa* is an interesting species with very few branches, mostly arising from the base and very erect. *H. rigidula,* on the other hand, is much-branched, forming a rounded outline, but decidedly upright-growing.

Some hebes start by growing upright when young, then become decumbent as they age, the branches falling over and growing more or less horizontally with the tips ascending. *H. hectorii* is one example, growing as a very erect plant with rigid stems when young, but often becoming decumbent after some years.

As you can see, the various shapes can be found in all sizes of hebes, from the tiny ones to the large border types. Depending on the spacing of the leaves on the branches, the sizes of the leaves, the length of branches, and the way the

branches grow, different effects are found even within each category. This shows what a versatile, varied group of plants the hebes are, and why they are so wonderful to use in all sorts of situations in the garden.

Winter foliage colour

As well as providing evergreen foliage, several hebes show distinct tints and colours in the leaves during colder weather. These can be invaluable during the winter, providing a focus among deciduous plants and giving you colour and interest in the border or rock garden. A group of hebes with coloured foliage can form a striking feature that is particularly attractive in winter. Try planting with bulbs and early-flowering plants, such as primroses, hellebores and cyclamen. Surround your winter-foliage hebes with toning or contrasting colours of bulbs: for example, yellow narcissi and tulips with *H. ochracea* 'James Stirling', adding mauve crocuses for contrast. Light or deep pink tulips will mirror the pinkish tints in the leaves of *H.* 'Primley Gem'. Plant in tubs or pots, together with bulbs, cyclamen, pansies or winter-flowering heathers, to provide colour near the house or in view of a window.

The maroon winter foliage colour of *Hebe* 'Red Edge'

Those with deeper hues in the foliage over winter also stand out well against plants with paler leaves, or those with grey or golden foliage.

Many hebes also have attractive colour in their young stems and shoots, which often intensifies as growth begins in early spring, giving quite striking effects. The red leaf margins of *H.* 'Red Edge' deepen in colour and extend to all the shoot tips, so the young shoots of the whole plant appear suffused with a deep maroon colour. The deep purple shoot tips of *H.* 'Caledonia', *H.* 'Heidi' and *H.* 'Blue Clouds' are outstanding in winter, while *H.* 'Autumn Glory' has a distinct purplish-red hue over much of its foliage. The shoot tips of *H.* 'Primley Gem' are flushed a pinkish colour, and *H.* 'County Park' is tinted pinkish-mauve, especially the young leaves and shoot tips.

Some hebes are surprisingly colourful in the depths of winter, their leaves almost glowing with reddish or purplish tints or flushes, even though they may be almost plain green during the summer. Others, such as those with bright green or yellowish-green foliage, stand out particularly well in winter, and can provide welcome spots of colour when everything around them may be either dull or dormant. Those with bright green, silvery-grey or golden foliage create splashes of colour among the winter garden, and are all the more valuable for this.

Hardiness

The majority of hebes, in particular the species plants, are hardy and capable of withstanding a certain amount of frost. Certainly, most of them can survive a normal winter in temperate areas such as southern England. In these sorts of areas, it is usually the larger, showy hybrids and cultivars that suffer from frost and cold weather, as these are rather more tender. Established plants are often better able to withstand a cold spell than newly planted ones, or those that are growing rapidly and consequently have softer growth. Many *H. speciosa* hybrids may suffer badly or succumb totally in a hard winter. Hebes that are less tender than these, but still susceptible, can be protected by mulching around the base, which allows buds below to shoot out in spring if the top growth is badly damaged or killed.

The tender types are likely to survive outside in mild areas, or in mild winters elsewhere. Reasonably hardy hebes can be damaged or cut back hard in a prolonged cold spell or sudden sharp frost; the larger-leafed types are more susceptible than those with smaller leaves. Planting in less exposed positions, or surrounded by other hardy plants, can diminish this risk. In any case, they often recover well. In cold areas, it is best to use really hardy types, which can withstand surprisingly low temperatures. Many hebes that are not hardy inland will, however, grow extremely well in coastal areas.

Variegated hebes are generally not at all hardy, particularly the large-leafed ones. However, we have found that they can withstand cold weather, notably when planted in a sheltered spot or with other evergreen plants around them. Alternatively, they can be planted in containers and moved into sheltered or frost-free conditions over the winter period.

The smaller and dwarf hebes are normally hardy or very hardy, surviving average winters with little or no damage. This generally includes those with smaller leaves and many of the whipcords and whipcord hybrids. Recently, new cultivars have been bred specifically for their hardiness as well as other attributes, so we now have some really good, more showy flowering hebes that are also hardy. Any frost-damaged growth on dwarf hebes can easily be cut out in spring, and it is usually only the tips or a few branches that are affected. In cold or exposed areas, it is advisable to plant only those hebes known to be really hardy and tough, though it is surprising what conditions some reasonably hardy types will come through. Again, it is helpful to plant them among other hardy plants for shelter. Look around your area and see which hebes are thriving in other gardens; this is an excellent indication of what will grow in your own garden.

The majority of hebes are capable of withstanding a certain amount of frost; this is *Hebe* 'Wiri Mist'

CHAPTER 2

Using hebes in the border

Evergreen structure planting

An evergreen backbone planting is important to the outline and structure of the garden, providing a framework around which you can build up colour schemes and groups of other plants. You can choose suitable hebes for background planting, as individual plants for effect, or as integral parts of a mixed border. Hebes are useful in mixed shrub borders both for their foliage and for their flowers. They have evergreen leaves, often with deeper tints in winter and on new young growth in spring. The medium- to large-sized hebes often flower in late summer and autumn when many other shrubs have finished blooming. Whatever sort of colour scheme or structure you are planning for a border, there is bound to be a suitable hebe to incorporate.

Hebes are excellent shrubs to use for providing structure and form in a border. The taller, large-flowered hebes can be planted towards the back, where they will form an evergreen backdrop to other shrubs and herbaceous plants, as well as putting on a display of flowers in summer and early autumn. In large borders there may be even

A large hebe adding structure and colour in the back of a border

This large hebe puts on a truly spectacular display outside a front door

Hebe 'White Gem' adds evergreen structure at the front of this border

Bright reddish-purple winter foliage of *Hebe* 'Autumn Glory'

taller shrubs or trees behind, in which case the hebes would form the middle planting. Give them plenty of space to develop fully, and make sure they are in a sunny position, and not overshadowed by larger plants.

Hebes are valuable among deciduous shrubs, providing evergreen foliage behind and among the bare branches in winter, and forming a background for emerging new leaves and buds in spring. Although often taken for granted, these backbone shrubs are all-important, the sheer bulk of branches and leaves lending structure and body to the border.

Many herbaceous plants are at their best during the summer; some have lush foliage and tall flowering stems, giving a blazing show of colour that adds immensely to the form of a mixed border. However, when these plants start to fade and die down for the winter, the whole border would look very stark and bare without the backbone of evergreen shrubs, which really do prove their worth at this time of the year.

Winter and early spring interest

Hebes are invaluable during the later part of the year for providing interest and colour in a border, whatever its size. The diversity of foliage colour, evergreen leaves and coloured stems and tips are valuable attributes of these shrubs. Individual hebes or groups can provide a striking winter feature or simply create some colour among deciduous and herbaceous plants.

Imagine brilliant red and yellow stems of deciduous shrubs planted together with the dark green, purple-flushed leaves of hebes. Use the coloured stems of *Cornus* (dogwood) among larger hebes or behind smaller types, or the dense red twigs of *Viburnum opulus* 'Nanum' with dwarf hebes. The coloured bark of some shrubs and trees can also be incorporated for effect. Red bark or stems can be stunning with silver foliage, so try planting these with some of the blue-grey or silvery hebes.

Even the green foliage of hebes varies considerably: it can be dark and sombre, fresh mid-green, bright emerald or soft yellowish-green. Many hebes have green leaves that are flushed purple or red in cold weather, or are lightly tinted on the margins most of the year, taking on more vivid colours in winter. These are particularly valuable for giving additional colour to the border. Try *H.* 'Blue Clouds', *H.* 'Red Edge' and *H.* 'Autumn Glory'.

Many show even more pronounced colouring as growth commences in early spring, the young shoot tips taking on a deep purple or maroon colour. *H.* 'Caledonia', *H.* 'Amy' and *H.* 'Sapphire' all have stunning winter coloration of deep purple young shoots and purplish tints on older leaves, giving an overall purple colour.

Remember that hebe foliage isn't just green. If you are planning a pastel border, use those with silvery-grey leaves. In sheltered gardens, you could add *H.* 'Dazzler' or *H.* 'Amanda Cook', with their largely pink- and mauve-tinted variegated leaves. Add ochre or golden touches with *H. ochracea* 'James Stirling' or *H. cupressoides* 'Golden Dome'.

Some hebes are notable for their coloured stems – even though these may not stand out as such, their cumulative effect with the colours of young leaves adds considerably to their interest. Some are purple or deep reddish-purple, while others are yellow or yellowish-green.

Rapid growth for new beds

When planting a new bed or border, you will probably want to get the backbone shrubs going as quickly as possible, to give you a structure to plant around. Then you can plan where to put

Deep purple winter coloration in young shoots of *Hebe* 'Amy'

other plants among them. Some hebes are capable of growing and establishing fairly rapidly, particularly those of large and medium size. Check that the forms you are planting are suitable for the space available. You need to know their ultimate size (both height and spread, as some grow wider than their height) to make sure they do not outgrow the space allotted to them in only a year or two.

Good initial preparation of the bed, and planting young, healthy, fast-growing plants, will help to make sure they grow away rapidly. Regular watering while establishing, as well as during dry spells, plus feeding and pruning at the appropriate times, will keep your new plants in peak condition and ensure that they grow away without check (more comprehensive details are given in Chapter 9).

Sizes

There are hebes suitable for any size garden, and for any size bed or border. Evergreen structure planting is just as important in a tiny front garden as in a huge border. You still need backbone planting or an evergreen framework, whether it consists of one or two plants or several.

Tall, large-leafed hebes are invaluable for the back of a border, and both tall and medium-sized bushy hebes are useful for planting among and behind deciduous and herbaceous plants or other evergreens. The small scale of dwarf hebes particularly suits the smaller gardens of many modern homes, and they are also ideal for the

Hebe 'Greensleeves' provides evergreen foliage and structure at the front of a border

front of a border or for any small bed. Choose the size of hebe to suit the scale of your border and the rest of your planting.

Low-growing hebes

Low-growing hebes are invaluable for providing evergreen foliage and structure at the front of a border. Many of these plants are neat and tidy in growth, but can still provide considerable variety. Choose the form, foliage colour and flower shades to fit in with the surrounding plants, and they will provide a framework as well as interest throughout the year. Globular forms include *H. topiaria* and *H.* 'Emerald Green', while *H.* 'Wiri Dawn' grows into a low mound. Others are low and sprawling, such as *H.* 'Petra's Pink'.

The spreading types will also grow over the edge of the bed, thereby softening the boundaries, and will merge with neighbouring low plants. This can be particularly effective when the plants involved have contrasting foliage: for example, grassy leaves, rounded foliage or matt, velvety leaves.

Hebe recurva is used to soften the edge of this border

Greenery behind plants, statues or containers

Hebes provide effective greenery when used as a backdrop to more colourful plants – not only do they continue looking good in winter when deciduous or herbaceous plants are bare or have died down, but they really show up the colourful flowers or foliage of other plants more effectively.

For example, golden flowers are always stunning against a dark green backdrop, and white flowers stand out particularly well in the same situation. Soft pink or lilac blooms look marvellous in front of deep purple or purple-flushed foliage; alternatively, they look well with silvery leaves. Silvery hebe foliage with white flowers looks cool and sophisticated, while primrose-yellow flowers associate happily with yellowish-green hebes. Make sure the flowers of the hebe itself are also compatible. Those with white, lilac or mauve flowers are fine with golden- and yellow-flowered plants, but take care that

pink-flowered hebes are planted to associate with more appropriate colours. These are most effective with plants that have flowers of white, lilac, mauve, purple or other pink shades.

Larger hebes form an effective background for other features in the garden, such as statues, planted containers and garden seating. A curtain of foliage around seats and statues has a softening effect, and statues in the border, whether figures, animals or stone birdbaths, are instantly more noticeable standing out against an evergreen shrub.

Hebes can also provide a background, whether growing in the soil or in a pot, for planted containers. They will provide interest and evergreen foliage all year round, plus flowers in season, while your planted containers develop or even move around during the year. Likewise, hebes are an effective backdrop for clumps of bulbs.

Planting combinations and associations

Both the foliage and the flowers of hebes combine successfully with a wide array of other plants in the border, and one variety or another can be found to fit into practically any border planting scheme. They are versatile among mixed groupings of plants, as background, as individual plants, or as ground cover. The rounded, bushy habit of many hebes provides solid blocks in a border to contrast with plants of strongly upright or prostrate outline. They can give substance and structure among more ephemeral or delicate plants, as well as providing all-year foliage among deciduous and herbaceous plants.

Use hebes as part of your framework in the border, combining with both evergreen and deciduous shrubs to give a structural backbone that you can subsequently fill in with other plants. If you are planting a shrub border, leave sufficient room around each shrub for it to develop a decent shape. Intersperse evergreen shrubs among deciduous ones, to provide some foliage throughout the border even in winter. In a mixed border, use larger hebes and other shrubs towards the back, with medium-sized plants in the centre and low ones at or near the front. Introduce suitable herbaceous perennials and grasses among them to give variation in shape, height and colour.

Hebe 'Wiri Mist' combined with other flowering plants in a colourful border

Hebe 'Baby Marie' brightening up a low bed

Considerations of shape

The more open, spreading hebes create space among denser plants. Those with small leaves, such as *H. pimeleoides* 'Quicksilver', can open up an area in the border, their widespread branches allowing more light and sun through so that smaller plants or bulbs can grow beneath them. Upright hebes, such as *H. pauciramosa* and *H.* 'James Platt', provide more vertical lines in a planting, and are useful in spaces where you don't want too much sideways growth, or where you need extra height among low-growing plants.

Prostrate and low-growing hebes add another dimension to a border, used either singly or in groups at the front. Some can form a weed-suppressing carpet, while others grow as low,

spreading hummocks. Use them to contrast with rounded bushes, upright plants and arching stems of foliage.

Similar effects can be achieved in either large or small-scale borders; there are hebes of various sizes, with different growth habits, which can be chosen according to the area you have available to fill.

Choose hebes with growth habits that suit you as well as your border – don't plant open, sprawling types if you can't bear anything out of place and you don't like informality in your plantings. There are plenty of neat, compact hebes if you prefer tidy plants that keep themselves within bounds. Conversely, if you have an informal border or a cottagey garden, extremely neat domes may look rather out of place, so choose hebes that are a little looser in habit, with stems that flow out from the plant or arch gracefully upwards. Solid domes of hebes can, however, provide excellent contrast to more informal, looser plants, so they can be successfully mixed in this way.

Colour combinations

Consider both foliage and flower colours when planning your border, or when adding a hebe to an existing border. Any plant looks better when it contrasts with or complements those plants surrounding it. Deep green hebes are enlivened by lighter foliage, so use plants with bright green, yellow-green, golden or silver foliage next to them. Variegated foliage stands out well against a dark backdrop. Fresh or bright green hebes associate brilliantly with golden leaves or flowers, or with gold and green variegated plants, or with purple or deep red foliage. They look wonderful surrounded by flowers of lilac, mauve or deep purple (such as asters, campanulas, geraniums), or cream, yellow or gold (such as coreopsis or helianthemums). They are also successful, in a quieter way, with all shades of pink and blue.

Silver and grey hebes give excellent contrast when planted among deep green foliage, and also look stunning with deep purple or red foliage, such as deciduous *Berberis* and some dahlias. They give a completely different effect when placed with pastel-coloured flowers and light foliage. Use them with pink, cream and purple variegated leaves (e.g. *Salvia officinalis* 'Tricolor'); purple-flushed foliage; cream, pink or lilac flowers. These are soft, harmonious colour schemes in which the silvery hebe blends in rather than standing out in stark contrast. A totally silver scheme can be achieved by planting with other silver plants, perhaps with

some white or soft mauve flowers. You will need different leaf textures and shapes for this to be really effective, such as the finely divided leaves of artemisias and the soft, silky leaves of *Convolvulus cneorum.*

The gold or ochre colour of some whipcord hebes looks wonderful with deep yellow, mauve and purple flowers. Whipcords provide great interest and contrast in a border, as their tiny leaves are held closely against the stem, giving them an almost conifer-like appearance. Place them next to plants with rounded, soft or toothed leaves, or with low carpeting plants around their base.

By using plants with golden leaves nearby or behind, the deep sombre colour of dark green and purple-tinged hebes can be given an immediate lift. This is even more effective when the hebe also has dark purple flowers, as these show up more against the brighter colour behind.

Hebes with white, lilac or purple flowers will associate with a huge range of plants, rarely causing any colour clashes or striking a jarring note in a colour scheme. Be more careful with pink-flowered hebes, as these would clash with yellow, orange or red-flowered plants. The deep pink-flowered hebes can look stunning against dark red or red-flushed foliage, but hot colours are best avoided against all pink-flowered hebes unless you are a particular fan of bright, clashing colours. There is nothing wrong in using all these colours in a mixed border, as long as there are sympathetically coloured plants between those that don't look so good together.

Many hebes flower over a long period, or have two or more flushes of flowers, so you need to be aware of the flower colours around at different times of the year. You could safely plant golden narcissi in front of a pink-flowered hebe if the latter was unlikely to flower before summer, as the bulbs would be long gone by then.

Combining with shrubs

Both deciduous and evergreen shrubs can be planted with hebes, using contrasting leaf shapes, textures and colours as well as flower shapes, colours and flowering periods, to give you as much interest as possible throughout the year.

Solid, bulky, evergreen shrubs are useful with open, sprawling hebes, providing contrast in shape and density. Use glossy leaves like those of *Escallonia* next to hebes with matt leaves; rounded, palmate or toothed leaves against long, slender hebe leaves; deep green or purple foliage with light green hebes; or golden shrubs (such as *Choisya ternata* 'Sundance', *Lonicera nitida* 'Baggesen's Gold') against dark green or purple hebes. Silvery shrubs such as *Santolina* or lavender are excellent displayed with purple-flushed hebes. Plant upright shrubs with rounded hebes; prostrate or groundcover shrubs in front of erect or bushy hebes; and open, spreading shrubs next to dense, dark hebe bushes. Shrubs with good, contrasting leaf shapes and textures include *Ceanothus*, *Cistus*, *Myrtus*, *Olearia* and *Osmanthus*.

Many deciduous shrubs are extremely floriferous, and excellent companions for hebes include *Caryopteris*, *Chaenomeles*, *Deutzia*, *Philadelphus*, *Potentilla* and hardy fuchsias. Others have interesting shapes or coloured winter stems that can be shown to advantage next to suitable hebes. Red-stemmed deciduous shrubs, for example, will appear to glow more brightly in front of hebes with dark green or purple-tinted leaves.

Hebe vernicosa provides a mound of colour in front of deciduous shrubs

Combining with perennials

Further textures and colours can be added to a mixed border by the use of herbaceous perennials. Although these die down almost completely in winter, they add fresh leaf growth in spring, then plenty of foliage and masses of flower during summer and autumn. They take up an amazing amount of space once in full growth, so leave sufficient room between your shrubs to accommodate them so that the shrubs do not become too swamped. Remember, hebes need plenty of light and an open position, so don't crowd them out in your border by trying to cram in too many plants.

Perennials have an incredible variety of foliage and flowers, so you have an enormous choice. Think of the tall, spear-like leaves of irises and crocosmias, and the strap-like foliage of *Hemerocallis* (day lilies), which are in stark contrast to the leaves and shape of hebes. Be careful with their flower colours, though; use soft yellows and blues with white and lilac hebes for a muted, hazy scheme, or orange and scarlet with deep purple hebe flowers to provide a striking contrast. The smoky colours of some irises harmonize beautifully with the foliage of ochre or purple-tinged hebes.

Alchemilla mollis and *Geranium renardii* have soft, felted leaves that look effective against shiny or leathery hebe leaves. Perennial geraniums are perfect around the base of medium- and large-sized hebes, as they don't mind some shade and will conceal the woody base. Some geraniums will even climb into the lower branches, creating a closer association, and the colours are generally sympathetic with those of hebes. Cut the geraniums back hard in late summer, when they tend to become straggly, to encourage fresh mounds of foliage.

The feathery foliage and pastel range of flowers of *Achillea* are excellent with hebes, while *Nepeta* and *Salvia* are good companions, with soft mauve or deep purple flowers over a long period in summer. Hellebores can add colour early in the year. The white flowers of *Helleborus niger* will brighten up dark hebes, while the dusky flowers of some *H. orientalis* hybrids blend beautifully with many others.

The white, pink and mauve shades of asters blend in very well with hebes, and they are available in a huge range of sizes, from dwarf ones of 25–35cm (10–14in) to use with small hebes, up to those of 1–1.2m (3ft 3in–4ft) in height for using further back in the border. The round, rayed flowers are in complete contrast to the spikes or racemes of hebes and, with appropriate choices, can be in flower together during late summer and autumn. Campanulas are also excellent with their bell- or cup-shaped flowers of white, mauve, blue or a pinkish shade. The tall stems of the bellflowers can gain shelter and support among hebes.

Winter interest

Evergreens are particularly valuable in a border largely full of deciduous shrubs and herbaceous perennials. In the winter months, the yellow-green tips of hebes such as *H. odora* 'New Zealand Gold' and *H. pauciramosa* really glow, standing out brightly against the soil, bare branches and any deep green evergreens. Hebes with reddish- or purple-flushed tips show up readily in winter. Bright green domes at the front of a border, such as *H.* 'Christabel' or *H.* 'Emerald Green', add solidity and freshness to a winter landscape, contrasting with any dark evergreens.

Late colour

Once early-flowering shrubs are over and summer perennials have been cut back, you will welcome the free-flowering nature of the many hebes that flower during late summer and autumn. They bring valuable colour and interest to the border late in the season, along with

Pink-flushed leaves of *Hebe* 'Primley Gem' form a harmonizing backdrop to this *Pulsatilla*

perennials such as asters and campanulas. Hebes with deep purple or violet flowers associate well with paler mauves and pinks, and those that have purple-tinged leaves add to this late colour. Pink-flowered hebes, usually fading to white to give a two-toned effect, look well with the soft colours of pink asters, white and blue parahebes and soft mauve scabious.

Late-flowering shrubs to use with hebes include *Abelia*, *Buddleja*, *Escallonia* 'Iveyi', *Myrtus*, *Olearia*, *Leycesteria*, *Ceratostigma*, *Perovskia* and *Caryopteris*. Many roses and hardy fuchsias are also valuable companions.

Use the flower colours of other plants to pick up any colours in hebe leaves. For example, pink flowers (tulips, violas, hellebores) will tone with the pinkish tints of *H*. 'Primley Gem' in winter and early spring, whereas mauve asters and crocuses will echo the deep violet flowers and purple-tinted leaves of *H*. 'Autumn Glory'.

Scrambling and climbing plants

To enliven larger, shrubby hebes during spring or add to their interest and colour in summer, you could try growing climbing or scrambling plants through their branches. Clematis and sweet peas are especially good grown among hebes.

Suitable species and varieties of clematis are excellent used in this way, and their flower colours tone really well with those of hebes, being mostly shades of pink, mauve and purple, together with white. Yellow-flowered clematis can be used with purple-flowered hebes, to provide a startling contrast. The best clematis to use, rather than the very large-flowered hybrids, are those with smaller flowers that look rather more dainty and in harmony.

Late-flowering clematis, such as Jackmanii varieties and *Clematis viticella* forms, are ideal on early summer-flowering hebes, extending the season of colour and interest considerably. These later-flowering clematis are pruned down hard in February every year, as new growth arises from the base and lower stems, so the hebe is clear of old woody growth. Plant on the shadiest side of the hebe so the roots of the clematis are in the coolest spot, and plant far enough away so the plants don't compete too much – and so that you can dig a deep enough hole to plant in. Mulch well each spring.

A *Clematis viticella* hybrid clambering through *Hebe* 'Amy'

This annual sweet pea (*Lathyrus articulatus*) scrambles through *Hebe* 'Primley Gem'

Sweet peas are lovely when left to scramble their way through hebes; their tendrils will cling round stems and leaves, and the flower stems are produced over a long period. It is worthwhile starting them off by training through the lower branches; then they can easily be left to cope for themselves. They will produce more flowers for longer if you regularly remove spent blooms.

Annual sweet peas are very effective used in this way and, like clematis, their flower colours blend beautifully with those of hebes. They can be raised from seed, either sown in the autumn and overwintered in a cold frame, or sown in the spring. There are many lovely named forms to choose from, including those with exquisite scent. You can also use the perennial climbing sweet pea, *Lathyrus latifolius* (often known as the 'everlasting pea'), which produces large flowers of pure white, pink or mauve on very long stems. Free-flowering over a long period, it can be more or less evergreen when grown in a sheltered position.

Lathyrus tingitanus is an easy annual species to grow, raised readily from seed, producing fast-growing stems up to 1.8–2.4m (6–8ft). It bears quite large purple, red-tinged flowers, and its leaves end in well-branched tendrils. You may also find *L. tingitanus* 'Roseus', with rose-pink and white flowers. Both are long-flowering and showy. Deadhead regularly to prolong the flowering season into autumn, and leave a few seed heads so you can collect the seed ready for the following year.

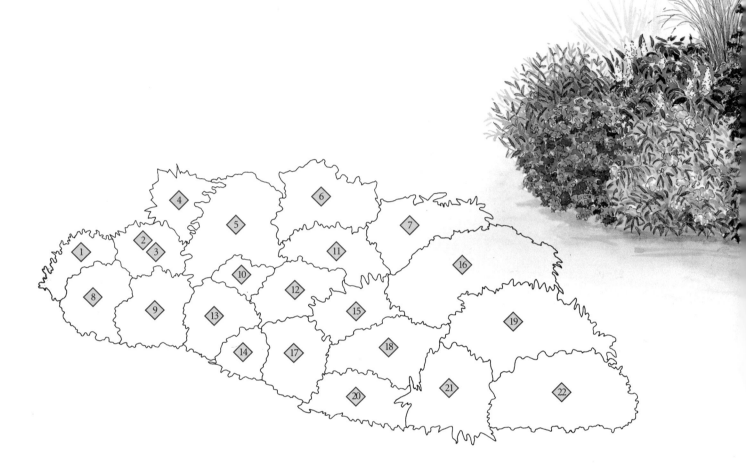

Plants

1 *Caryopteris × clandonensis* 'Heavenly Blue'

2 *Hebe* 'Spender's Seedling'

3 *Clematis viticella* 'Etoile Violette'

4 *Miscanthus sinensis* 'Graziella'

5 *Berberis thunbergii* f. *atropurpurea*

6 *Escallonia* 'Iveyi'

7 *Hebe* 'Lopen'

8 *Geranium × magnificum*

9 *Cistus* 'Silver Pink'

10 *Anemone × hybrida* 'Whirlwind'

11 *Hebe* 'Alicia Amherst'

12 *Potentilla fruticosa* 'Tilford Cream'

13 *Aster × frikartii* 'Mönch'

14 *Parahebe perfoliata*

15 *Hebe* 'Bowles's Hybrid'

16 *Choisya* 'Aztec Pearl'

17 *Hebe* 'Margret'

18 *Cistus × corbariensis*

19 *Hebe* 'Blue Clouds'

20 *Dianthus* 'Diane'

21 *Veronica spicata* 'Alba'

22 *Geranium clarkei* 'Kashmir White'

Large mixed border (part of)

Illustrated in midsummer

Planted for year-round interest and colour, this border contains a variety of evergreen and deciduous shrubs and herbaceous perennials, and includes a number of different hebes. Plants are placed to emphasize the variety of habit, foliage and flowers. A clematis scrambles through one of the hebes, and the planting has a harmonizing colour scheme with flowers of white, cream, silvery-pink, blue, violet and purple against a background that includes glossy green, purple and variegated foliage. The flowering season lasts from early summer right through until late autumn.

Small mixed border

Illustrated in early summer

This small border in front of a low wall contains hebes and a variety of other dwarf plants, showing how a range of foliage types and plant shapes can be successfully combined. It has been designed to give a succession of flowering from mid-spring until mid-autumn. Leaves are silver, glaucous and pale grey-green as well as green, and the flowers are soft colours of pink, lilac, cream and white.

Plants

1. *Hebe hulkeana*
2. *Convolvulus cneorum*
3. *Lavandula angustifolia* 'Imperial Gem'
4. *Hebe colensoi*
5. *Hebe* 'Wiri Dawn'
6. *Helianthemum* 'Wisley White'
7. *Teucrium fruticans* 'Compactum'
8. *Hebe* 'Wiri Cloud'
9. *Iris* 'Blue Pools'
10. *Hebe* 'Petra's Pink'
11. *Festuca glauca* 'Elijah Blue'
12. *Potentilla nepalensis* 'Miss Willmott'
13. *Deutzia crenata* var. *nakaiana* 'Nikko'
14. *Diascia* 'Lilac Belle'
15. *Aster novi-belgii* 'Lady in Blue'
16. *Geranium sanguineum* var. *striatum*
17. *Hebe amplexicaulis* f. *hirta*
18. *Helianthemum* 'Sudbury Gem'

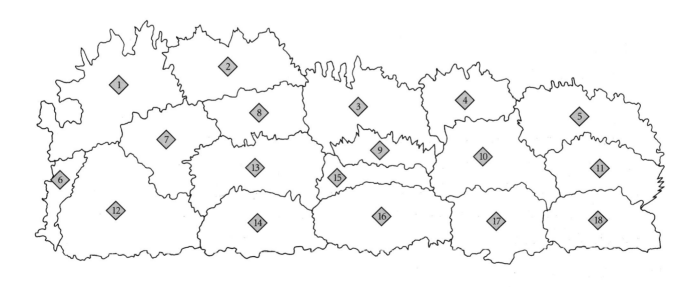

CHAPTER 3

Rock gardens and raised beds

The slow growth or naturally dwarf habit of many hebes means that they are well suited to planting in rock gardens and raised beds. There are a number of tiny or small hebes to use for structure, foliage and flower interest in small-scale features, while an even wider choice is available for larger rock gardens.

Hebes make an effective evergreen backbone to a rock-garden planting, in a similar way to dwarf conifers. They provide a constant background for the array of colourful alpines planted in rock gardens, lending additional colour and interest by means of their own foliage and flowers. They continue to look good throughout the winter when many alpines have died down or been trimmed back. Hebes can also stand as specimen plants in a rock garden, in a pocket of their own, while still contributing to the overall effect. The majority of alpines tend to flower during spring and early summer, so any hebes with particularly attractive foliage or with a later flowering period are especially valuable.

(Opposite) *Hebe cupressoides* 'Boughton Dome' is suitable for a large rock garden or raised bed

(Below) The neat form of *Hebe buchananii* is ideal for providing structure in a raised bed

rocks, and is valuable for its early blooming. If you have room, plant in a group of three or five for more impact. *H.* 'Youngii' is a popular low, spreading shrublet with pretty violet flowers, ideal for introducing a carpet of bright colour. Another well-known plant is *H. pinguifolia* 'Pagei', with mounds of grey-green leaves smothered in white flowers during late spring.

Choose colours and shapes to contrast or harmonize with neighbouring plants, and always trim back after flowering to tidy and encourage fresh growth.

How to use hebes

Hebes can be used as background for other small plants, and as structural elements, forming part of the backbone of a planting. Their evergreen foliage is all-important in this role, and both erect and

Foliage hebes

Excellent foliage types include the slow-growing dwarf whipcords and whipcord hybrids, such as *H.* 'Emerald Green', *H.* 'Christabel', *H.* 'Loganioides' and *H. lycopodioides*. Choose *H.* 'Greensleeves' if you want flowers as well, because this is unusual among whipcord types in being free with its flowers, producing many white spikes. On larger rock gardens, you can use *H. ochracea* 'James Stirling', a wonderful addition on account of its old-gold foliage colour, and *H. cupressoides* 'Boughton Dome', a dense hummock of mainly juvenile foliage. These are both slow-growing but do eventually reach a size that would be out of proportion in a small-scale planting.

Flowering hebes

Recommended flowering hebes that are small in stature include *H.* 'Baby Marie', which benefits from the shelter that can be provided between

Colourful buds of *Hebe* 'Baby Marie'

bushy forms can add much-needed height to a rock garden or raised bed. The inclusion of a few taller plants such as these can help to balance a planting of carpeting, hummock-shaped and low, tufted alpines.

Alternatively, use small, low-growing or prostrate hebes as ground cover, where the carpeting effect of stems and leaves provides a foil for shrubby or upright alpines. Hebes with trailing stems can be strategically placed so that they gradually grow over rock faces, or down the sides of a raised bed, in order to soften the hard outlines. Dome-shaped hebes contrast with spiky or upright alpines, and also look good with carpeting alpines, such as thymes and veronicas, around them.

Prostrate hebes can form effective cover for dwarf bulbs. Plant clumps of miniature or dwarf spring bulbs around the base of the hebe, and they will grow up through the branches, producing a colourful show at flowering time above the hebe foliage. Use a variety of bulbs if you want a succession of flowers, or a number of the same sort for a mass display. Crocuses, dwarf narcissi, scillas, puschkinias and small species tulips are all effective grown in this way. The hebe stems and foliage start to grow away again in spring, so by the time the bulbs are coming to an end, the bulb foliage can be at least partially hidden among the new hebe growth. Leave the bulb foliage to die down naturally, and pull away once completely dead and brown. Each year the bulbs should increase and spread, as the hebe grows larger, to give you an increasingly colourful display. Bulbs can either be planted at the same time as the hebe – in which case you can push them in fairly close to the main stem – or you can add them later by pushing them in under the hebe branches.

The trailing stems of *Hebe chathamica* can soften hard edges and surfaces

You may use hebes as dwarf bulb cover on either small or large rock gardens or raised beds; try *H.* 'Youngii' for a small feature, or *H.* 'County Park' or *H.* 'Wingletye' on a larger area.

Larger rock gardens can accommodate hebes up to 40–60cm (16–24in) or so in height, bearing in mind that many also grow as wide as, or even wider than, their height. Those with small leaves, well clothed in foliage and remaining fairly compact and neat, are more suitable, forming good backbone shrubs and definite shapes within the rock garden. The same principles regarding contrast in shape and colour apply as they do to small rock gardens. However, on larger features you do have more scope, with bigger groupings of plants.

Whether you are planting just a few, or several hebes, aim to include bushes of different shapes. Use low-growing types such as *H.* 'Youngii', *H.* 'Petra's Pink' and *H. amplexicaulis* f. *hirta* as ground cover, or for trailing over or covering rock faces. Bun-shaped forms such as *H.* 'Jasper' or *H.* 'Emerald

Green' add solidity and structure, and provide contrast to carpeting or spiky alpines. Bushy forms like *H. recurva* and *H.* 'Baby Marie', and upright growers such as *H. hectorii*, add height and bulk.

Choose an assortment of hebes for your rock garden or raised bed to give you flowers over a long season. A well-chosen selection could provide you with a display from mid-spring right through until late summer, the period during which most dwarf hebes flower. Remember that some hebes have a short burst of flowers, while others have a succession of blooms over many weeks. As an example, *H. buchananii* and *H.* 'Jasper' could follow the early-flowering *H. raoulii* var. *pentasepala* and *H.* 'Baby Marie'. The flowers of *H.* 'Petra's Pink' would continue the display, followed by *H. recurva* and *H.* 'Pimeba' into late summer.

Attractive white flowers of *Hebe* 'Jasper'

Drainage

The amount of drainage provided in rock gardens and raised beds is worth a mention, as many of these features are built specifically to give particularly good drainage for alpines. Rock gardens can become quite dry on the upper parts, as water will drain down into the lower parts and the soil beneath. Raised beds are often extremely well drained, their bases being filled with broken crocks, rubble or gravel, and the soil within the bed having additional grit to provide suitable growing conditions for alpines. You need to be careful not to plant hebes in areas prone to excessive drying out, as they won't tolerate dryness at the roots, and you may find it difficult to establish them in these conditions.

Hebes are best planted at or near the base of rock gardens, or in places where the roots can grow underneath rocks, where the soil will be cool and retain more moisture. Make sure you water newly planted hebes thoroughly both at planting time and for some time afterwards, until they are established and growing strongly. Once their roots are growing well down into the soil, they have a far greater chance of success.

Raised beds often have a top dressing of grit once planted, and this can help to retain moisture by preventing rapid evaporation from the soil surface. Again, it is advisable to water newly planted hebes regularly, particularly during dry spells, so that their roots can grow down into the soil. If the bed is built on a soil base, the roots will find their way through the drainage layer at the base and into the soil below, which will give them a greater reservoir of water to tap into. In order to encourage the roots to find their way down, don't just sprinkle water little and often over the plant, as this will only penetrate a tiny way into the soil and

The whipcord foliage of this hebe contrasts with colourful alpines

Hebe 'Edinensis' adds height to mat-forming alpines

roots will just develop near the surface. Give the plant a thorough watering so that water travels well down into the soil; this encourages the roots to delve down to search for water.

Raised beds built on a solid surface, such as concrete, will inevtiably be more susceptible to drying out, as the soil available is limited to that within the bed itself. However, take care to water your hebes, both when establishing them and in any dry spells, and you should be able to grow them successfully.

Combining hebes with other small plants

For a small rock garden or raised bed, choose neat, dwarf hebes and slow-growing, compact alpines and miniature conifers; otherwise the area will become overrun in no time.

Low-growing hebes contrast with bushy and tufted alpines such as pinks, asters and shrubby thymes, and with conical or globular conifers. Bushy hebes add height to mat-forming campanulas, veronicas and sedums. Both flower and foliage colours can be chosen to contrast or complement, and to give you bright or soft colour schemes.

Here are some suggestions:

◆ *Hebe* 'Loganioides', with bronze-tinted whipcord foliage, associates with dwarf blue *Aquilegia flabellata* 'Ministar' and miniature golden narcissi in spring; a mat-forming, variegated *Arabis* adds bright foliage colour. Deep blue *Campanula*, white *Dianthus* and soft mauve thymes harmonize with the violet flowers of *Hebe* 'Youngii' in summer, and this whole group provides a variety of form, foliage and colour. For a brighter colour scheme, plant scarlet *Penstemon pinifolius* with *Hebe* 'Youngii', or rose-pink helianthemums with grey-leafed *Hebe pinguifolia* 'Pagei'.

◆ A larger rock garden could have *Hebe cupressoides* 'Boughton Dome' surrounded by carpets of mauve *Campanula*, pink *Scutellaria pontica* and silver-leafed *Antennaria*, together with colourful helianthemums and *Armeria maritima* with its grassy leaves and pink thrift flowers.

To add further variety, there are conical, globular and flat-topped dwarf conifers, and suitable shrubs include *Berberis × stenophylla* 'Corallina Compacta', *Deutzia crenata* var. *nakaiana* 'Nikko' and *Potentilla* 'Sungold'. Small forms of *Festuca*, *Carex* and other ornamental grasses can add interest with their foliage form and colour.

Rock garden (part of)

Illustrated in early summer

A selection of whipcord hebes and neat flowering hebes associates beautifully with colourful flowering alpines, together providing a display of white, pink, deep pink and blue flowers from late spring to late summer.

Trailing and carpeting alpines are an invaluable way to soften the hard appearance of the rock surfaces, while the low, bushy hebes add a structural backbone and interesting foliage.

Plants

◇1 *Hebe* 'Edinensis'

◇2 *Dianthus* 'Dewdrop'

◇3 *Hebe cupressoides* 'Boughton Dome'

◇4 *Thymus* 'Porlock'

◇5 *Hebe carnosula*

◇6 *Hebe* 'Christabel'

◇7 *Hebe* 'Youngii'

◇8 *Sedum spurium* 'Purpurteppich'

◇9 *Scutellaria alpina*

◇10 *Achillea* 'Huteri'

◇11 *Hebe buchananii*

◇12 *Parahebe lyallii* 'Julie-Anne'

◇13 *Campanula carpatica* 'Blaue Clips'

◇14 *Dianthus* 'La Bourboule'

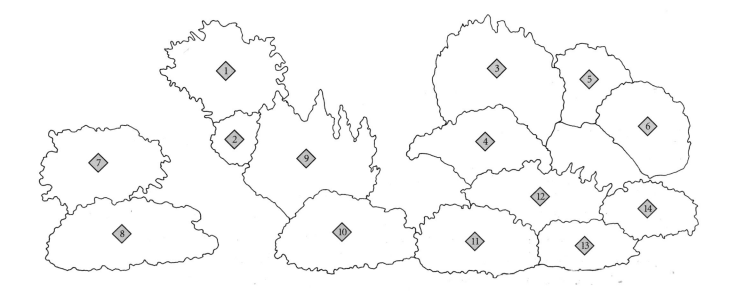

Raised bed (part of)

Illustrated in late spring

A low brick raised bed, filled with a well-drained soil mix and topped with chippings, holds a collection of dwarf hebes and alpines to provide both evergreen structure and a colourful display for much of the year. Most of the hebes have flowers as well as interesting foliage, and they are surrounded by mound-forming, trailing and tufted alpines with flowers of deep blue, mauve, pink and white.

The plants are arranged so as to exploit these contrasting shapes and foliage to maximum effect.

Plants

1. *Iris* 'Knick Knack'
2. *Campanula garganica*
3. *Hebe* 'Jasper'
4. *Veronica pinnata* 'Blue Eyes'
5. *Dianthus* 'Dainty Dame'
6. *Hebe* 'Emerald Green'
7. *Veronica prostrata* 'Rosea'
8. *Sisyrinchium idahoense*
9. *Geranium dalmaticum*
10. *Saponaria* × *olivana*
11. *Anacyclus pyrethrum* var. *depressus*
12. *Phyteuma scheuchzeri*
13. *Gypsophila repens* 'Fratensis'
14. *Hebe raoulii* var. *pentasepala*
15. *Oxalis adenophylla*
16. *Hebe epacridea*
17. *Antennaria microphylla*

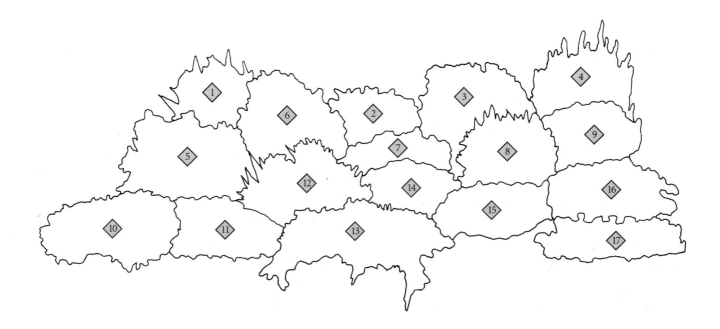

Hebe 'Wingletye' can be used for effective ground cover

CHAPTER 4

Ground cover and edging

Plants are used as ground cover in order to form a canopy over the soil, sufficiently dense to prevent weeds growing through. Low, spreading plants are ideal, as they cover the ground and block out light beneath them, making it difficult for weed seeds to germinate. Competition for water and nutrients also hinders weed growth.

There are a number of hebes that are very useful for covering either small patches or larger areas of ground. A single hebe can be used to effect at the front of a border, for example, or perhaps planted on the corner of a bed, or in any place where a low-growing shrub is required. At the other extreme, large tracts of ground can be filled with one or more varieties of prostrate or low mounded hebes to form attractive, effective weed-smothering ground cover.

The evergreen nature of hebes makes them an excellent choice for ground cover, and any forms with attractively coloured leaves or good flowers can be particularly valuable. They are generally easy to grow, establishing fairly rapidly, and, on a large scale, would require only moderate pruning to maintain tidiness. Some can provide quite dense cover, ideal for minimizing weed growth.

There are other advantages in using hebes for ground cover. Apart from being clothed in foliage all year round, they are long-lasting, permanent plants.

They don't get out of control, as do many commonly used ground-cover plants. Periwinkle (*Vinca*) and rose of Sharon (*Hypericum calycinum*), often planted to cover large areas or banks, send shoots up all over the place from running underground stems, spreading out a great distance from the main plant, and can become difficult to control.

Low-growing hebes are also effective for use as edging, either planted in a row along the front of a border or the edge of a bed, or placed in small groups to define a boundary or an outline. Use them alongside a drive, pathway or patio, where they will soften the hard edges without spreading over too much. Simply trim regularly after flowering to keep the plants within bounds, and they will provide you with a neat, attractive edge all year round.

Hebe pinguifolia 'Pagei' provides effective ground cover on the corner of this border

Ground cover

Which hebes to use

The obvious types of hebe to use for ground cover are those with a naturally prostrate habit, such as *H.* 'Wingletye', *H.* 'County Park' and *H. albicans* 'Sussex Carpet'. It is also worth considering those low-growing hebes that form compact or more wide-spreading domes or mounds with a good covering of foliage; *H. chathamica* and *H.* 'Wiri Dawn' are two examples. Some decumbent hebes are useful, as their branches spread more or less outwards, with just the tips turning skywards, so they can give adequate soil cover. *H. decumbens* and *H.* 'Youngii' can both be used successfully.

Any of these types can be used either individually as a ground-cover specimen in a border or rock garden, or planted as a group for weed-smothering purposes.

Hebe 'Youngii' is a smaller ground-cover hebe

On a larger scale, taller hebes can be effective planted en masse, particularly if they have dense, compact growth well-clothed in small leaves, and are planted close enough so that they eventually completely cover the area. You often see this sort of planting in towns and public areas, and it can look attractive when well maintained. *H.* 'White Gem' and *H. rakaiensis* are commonly seen planted in this way. These dome-shaped hebes often have a girth wider than their height, spreading out more or less symmetrically to create cushions of foliage.

Low mounded hebes

An individual specimen of a low, bushy hebe is ideal for filling a space in a small bed or at the front of a border. The plant's habit means that it will cover the soil effectively, and eventually help to inhibit weed growth, particularly if the hebe is pruned regularly to keep it bushy and clothed with foliage as near to ground level as possible. If allowed to become leggy, it will be less dense and therefore less effective. Any fairly low hebe with a compact habit, relatively close foliage covering, with a bushy branching habit or mounded, cushion-like shape, will happily fulfil this function. Good examples include *H.* 'Wiri Dawn', with slender, light green leaves and elegant rose-pink flowers, and *H.* 'Margret', which has sky-blue flowers over mounds of shiny foliage.

This type of hebe can also be attractive planted in groups; a group of three may be sufficient in a small garden for an effective area of ground cover, while in a larger area you will need greater numbers. By staggering the planting (placing the hebes irregularly rather than in rows), you will create a denser covering more quickly. The hebes will grow out towards each other and eventually meet to form a continuous canopy.

Hebe pinguifolia 'Pagei' forms dense ground cover

Prostrate hebes

Prostrate and decumbent hebes vary in the way
they grow. Some form close-knit, well-branched
mats covered in closely overlapping small leaves,
while others have a more open structure. They vary
in their spread, some being slow-growing and
compact, others spreading widely and more rapidly.

- *H. pinguifolia* 'Pagei' is an excellent low ground-cover plant, forming dense weed-suppressing mats of rounded grey-green foliage, the stems covered in leaves and held close to the ground, sometimes rooting into the soil as it grows. It is lovely in any pink-blue-purple colour scheme, or with silver and white plants.
- *H.* 'County Park' grows faster and is more wide-spreading, though still densely clothed and with colourful winter foliage.
- *H. albicans* 'Sussex Carpet' has long branches spreading widely, overlapping each other in layers. The leaves are more widely spaced on the branches, but this layered effect gives good cover.
- *H.* 'Wingletye' forms a dense mat of well-clothed spreading stems, the glaucous leaves toning beautifully with the lilac flowers.

Colour

Use the leaf colour of ground-cover hebes to add interest to your planting schemes. The blue-grey forms are attractive and will lighten any planting, looking less sombre than a carpet of dark green. The bright green mounded hebes also add a lighter touch, for example *H. chathamica* and *H.* 'Wiri Dawn'. You could use varieties such as *H.* 'Youngii' and *H.* 'County Park' to add more colour in winter as, during cold weather, their foliage takes on deeper tints of reddish-purple and pinkish-purple respectively.

The dark foliage of *Hebe* 'Petra's Pink' provides contrasting ground cover in front of *H. albicans*

A carpet of hebes can be created on a larger scale by using different ground-cover varieties, providing a tapestry of varying colours of leaves and flowers. This can be extremely attractive, say, on a large bank or island bed, or any large expanse that needs ground-cover plants, or where you may like a relatively easy planting that looks good all year. A mixture of the ground cover types *H. albicans* 'Sussex Carpet', *H.* 'County Park', *H.* 'Wingletye', *H. pinguifolia* 'Pagei' and *H. chathamica* will provide a range of foliage and flower colours as well as attractive winter leaf colour.

Position and pruning

Hebes used for ground cover still require an open, sunny position to grow in, so it is no use expecting to use them as a carpet under trees or conifers, or beneath large shrubs, as they simply won't receive sufficient light. Use them instead at the front of a border, in open spaces in beds, or on other open expanses of soil, such as banks. In small areas, you will need to prune regularly to maintain them and keep them within bounds; this also keeps the plants bushier and well clothed in foliage, with new shoots growing out from nearer the centre of the shrub rather than just at the tips. For instance, *H.* 'County Park' readily produces new growth from the centre once pruned, whereas it can become bare and leggy if left.

On large areas, plants can be allowed to spread more freely in order to cover the soil more thoroughly; but you should still prune them at least every so often, or the plants are liable to become leggy and develop bare patches in the centre.

Spacing

Groups of ground-cover hebes are effective weed smotherers, their overlapping branches and close-set leaves helping to cut out the light beneath them. As they grow and intermingle, they will form a dense cover which, being evergreen, is effective all year round. The planting distance between hebes depends on the variety used and the density of cover required. A spacing of 25–40cm (10–16in) is usually sufficient to create effective ground cover while giving each plant room to grow. If you have a large area to fill, you can space wide-spreading or mixed ground-cover hebes up to 60cm (2ft) apart, but they will take longer to merge together, and meanwhile uncovered areas need to be kept weed-free.

Edging

We have already mentioned the effectiveness of low-growing hebes for use as edging. They are ideal for softening the hard edges of paths and driveways. Use them alongside any kind of path, whether concrete, flagstones, brick or gravel, as long as there is sufficient room for them to grow without narrowing the path too much. Hebes can also be planted alongside a driveway to soften its appearance, whether you have just a short length or a longer, wider expanse. These hard landscaped areas need foliage to lessen their stark impact, and low hebes are an excellent choice, with their attractive appearance all year round, coupled with their compact, neat shape.

Other areas in which to use hebes for edging are those awkward, often very narrow, strips of border between neighbouring gardens, frequently found between drives or paths in front gardens.

If there is a fence between the two, the strip may still be wide enough to plant dwarf hebes, as long as it is not in the shade of a solid fence. If there is no fence, and your neighbours are in agreement, the whole strip planted with dwarf hebes can look most attractive, and form a delineation between the two gardens.

Many gardens also have narrow borders running alongside a fence or wall, either in the front or back garden, and, so long as these are not north-facing, they can be usefully planted with an edging of dwarf or low-growing hebes. Varieties with attractive foliage add to the interest, as do flowering types.

Some useful combinations for low edging

◆ *H. carnosula*, with grey-green, thick, fleshy leaves and short, rounded white flowers, and trailing *Gypsophila repens* in front.
◆ *H. decumbens*, with shiny green leaves on purple-black stems and pretty white flowers, plus *Sedum spurium* 'Purpurteppich' or *Thymus serpyllum* 'Russetings'.
◆ *H. pinguifolia* 'Pagei', with grey-green leaves and white flowers, plus *Veronica prostrata* (deep blue) or *V. prostrata* 'Rosea' (pink).

An edging can be made up of several plants of the same hebe variety, or a mixture of two or three different ones in groups. A single variety can give a more formal look, and is also best if you prefer a simpler, plainer approach. For a more informal look, or to add further colour and interest, we suggest using two or three varieties in groups, depending on the length you are planting, and choosing different foliage and flower colours. A selection of grey-green, silvery and purplish hebes ensures plenty of variety, and will look colourful even when not in flower. Choose a combination of white and lilac or purple flowers, and you will be assured of a tapestry of subtle colouring all year round, particularly once the plants start to intermingle a little as they establish. They are best planted in groups of at least three, and preferably more on larger areas, so that the edging does not appear as a random series of dots.

A neat edging of *Hebe topiaria* softens and delineates this boundary

Suitable edging hebes
30–40cm (12–16in) in height

♦ *H. vernicosa* will form a bushy edging with glossy foliage and pale lilac flowers. For a mixed edging, combine with *H. albicans* or *H.* 'Pewter Dome', both with grey-green leaves, or *H. recurva*, with grey foliage. All these have white flowers. *H.* 'Margret', with shiny bright green leaves and sky-blue flowers, would also look attractive.

For a long row of edging plants, you could repeat the alternating groups either at regular intervals, or more randomly, to give waves of differing colour along the length. This sort of edging is best if the varieties used are similar in growth habit and height, so that the effect is more or less even.

Edging borders

Edging is also useful along borders, either for definition or to keep other plants in the border from flopping over onto lawns and paths. Dwarf or low mounded hebes can make a neat border edging that looks good even in winter. Use either a single row, or a double, staggered row if you have room, allowing the plants to merge into each other around their sides to form a continuous band of foliage. If you prefer, you can keep each plant as a discrete mound, which will still give you a neat edge; trim each plant to more or less equal size, or the edging will look messy and uneven.

Further interest and variety can be introduced by the inclusion of other low plants in front of the hebe edging if there is room – in particular carpeting or spreading types such as thymes or sedums. If you plant these at the same time as the hebes, put them in alternately but slightly further forward, so that they fill up the gaps and the area in front of the hebes. The carpeting plants can spill over the edge, and will create additional colour. Use purple-leafed sedums or prostrate thymes with soft flower colours of pink, mauve or white, or mat-forming veronicas with their spikes of blue or pink flowers.

Pruning

Hebe edging should be pruned regularly, partly to keep the plants bushy and compact, but also to keep the edging neat, even and tidy. You don't want the plants sprawling out over your path, driveway or lawn, with leggy branches getting in the way and being trodden on. It is far better to get into the habit of trimming them regularly, once or twice a year, so you don't have a major job to get them back into shape. Prune flowering hebes immediately after flowering has finished, to encourage new shoots to grow out. Trim evenly round each plant, or along all sides and the top of an established continuous edging. If you want a less even appearance, as with a mixed hebe edging perhaps, you can be less rigid in the evenness of your trimming, aiming instead for a looser, more informal look.

Slightly taller hebes used as an edging in front of a fence or wall can just be pruned as normal, after flowering, by up to one third, without making them too formal and even.

CHAPTER 5

Hebe beds

A colourful bed filled entirely with hebes

The immense variety to be found among hebes makes them eminently suitable for planting a whole bed or border entirely with different varieties of hebe. By placing contrasting shapes and colours next to each other, it is very easy to create an interesting, colourful border. Choosing hebes to give you as long a flowering season as possible will add to the long-term interest. An imaginative use of plant shapes, together with different leaf sizes, textures and colours, and variation in flower colour and flowering periods, can provide you with a permanent feature of much interest all year round.

A hebe bed, like any shrub border, is particularly valuable if you wish to create a permanent planting that requires little maintenance beyond regular pruning and tidying. Having no perennials or bulbs dispenses with all the necessary clearing of spent flowers and foliage, and leaves no bare gaps during autumn and winter where these have died down.

A bed devoted to hebes is not at all monotonous; on the contrary, the juxtaposition of various forms and colours can be immensely pleasing to the eye, from a distance as well as close up. There are so many fine species and hybrids available that it is possible to create all sorts of interesting designs, whether you are planting a tiny bed, a large border or anything in between.

Choose effective combinations of foliage and shape, as in this group of *Hebe ochracea* 'James Stirling', *H.* 'Wiri Mist' and *H.* 'Sapphire'

Points to consider

The art of creating a really interesting tapestry of hebes lies firstly in the choice of the plants, and secondly in combining them to display each to its best effect. Much of the advice on mixed borders in Chapter 2 – about placing plants together with regard to their shape and colour – is also relevant to hebe beds. The primary consideration should be the appearance of the foliage, as this is on display all year round, and will form the basis of your hebe bed. At the same time, think about the growth habit of those you have chosen, and arrange them accordingly so that neighbouring

One of the earliest-flowering varieties, *Hebe* 'Baby Marie'

plants enhance one another. Make sure, also, that each has sufficient room to develop its natural shape. A bushy, rounded hebe often grows wider than its height, whereas an erect hebe takes up much less room sideways. Prostrate and decumbent hebes, on the other hand, have very little height but do take up more ground space. Don't assume, therefore, that you can just plant your hebes at equal distances apart, otherwise some will rapidly encroach over the space occupied by slower or less spreading ones.

It is less important to take flower colour into account in hebe beds than in a mixed border, because all hebe flower colours are compatible – white, pink, lilac, mauve and purple. The choice falls to your own personal taste, but unless you want just one colour, such as white, it is preferable to try and spread the different colours throughout the bed. Consider the flowering period of each hebe, remembering that while some have a fleeting season, others bloom over an extended period of some months. Flower shapes vary considerably, too; some are short, dense and compact, such as *H. albicans*, while others are long and graceful as in *H.* 'Alicia Amherst'.

Choose varieties to suit the scale of the bed you are planting. There are numerous dwarf forms for small-scale planting, so you can create a small hebe bed with just as much colour and interest as you can a large border using taller or bushier hebes. You can also mix different sizes in a bed, with shorter ones near the front, or just use shorter varieties by themselves in a large bed. It all depends on the effect you want to achieve.

Hebe 'Nicola's Blush' continues to flower over many months

Foliage interest

Hebes with attractive foliage give a much longer season of interest. The diversity of foliage colour and the coloured stems and young growths of many, as well as their being evergreen, are extremely valuable attributes of these shrubs. The range of leaf colours is all the more impressive when you place hebes near to each other: the numerous shades of green, grey-green and blue-grey are amazing. In addition, many hebes take on coloured tints, or more pronounced colour, during cold weather, which adds considerably to their appeal during winter and early spring. Others have variegated foliage, such as *H.* 'Glaucophylla Variegata' with its tiny, pale cream and grey-green leaves, or the much larger *H.* 'Lopen', which has bright green leaves broadly edged with creamy yellow. Some variegated hebes, like *H.* 'Pink Elephant' and *H.* 'Dazzler', become suffused with burgundy or pinkish-purple in cold weather. There are also the more unusual whipcord hebes and their hybrids, with tiny scale-like leaves adding textural interest.

Leaf structure

The diversity of size, shape and colour in hebe foliage makes it almost impossible not to choose an interesting mixture of plants. Tiny leaves clustered closely on the stems and long, willowy, slender leaves are two extremes of leaf structure, with a huge range of sizes and shapes in between (usually more or less in proportion to the size of the plant). Consider the contrast of leaf shapes, sizes and textures: leaves may be large or tiny; flat or curved;

An attractive foliage combination, with *Hebe* 'Glaucophylla Variegata', *H.* 'Caledonia' and *H.* 'Primley Gem'

shiny, matt or leathery. Think of the long, willowy leaves of *H. salicifolia* adjacent to the large, broad leaves of *H.* 'Alicia Amherst'; or the small, glossy leaves of *H. vernicosa* contrasting with the more rounded, thick, concave leaves of *H. carnosula*.

The diverse leaf shapes of *Hebe* 'Bowles's Hybrid', *H. hectorii* and *H. decumbens*

Winter colour

Hebes with coloured or tinted foliage are excellent for winter interest, complementing the plain green-leafed forms. Those hebes that take on even more vivid colour in the winter months should be planted and used more often. In summer, H. 'Red Edge' is merely a neat bush of grey-green, red-rimmed leaves, but in winter it becomes suffused with maroon, which deepens in colour over much of the leaf surface and transforms it into a truly striking plant.

H. 'Blue Clouds' also takes on deep purple colouring in winter, particularly in the tips and the younger leaves, and H. 'Sapphire' becomes a much darker purple. The slightly pinkish-purple tinge of H. 'Primley Gem' foliage spreads further over the leaf surface in cold weather, transforming its appearance. H. 'Autumn Glory' has dark purple tips and young leaves in winter, which look even more striking if some of its deep violet flowers are lingering late in the year. The plain green leaves of H. 'Nicola's Blush' are decidedly bronze-tinged in a cold winter, as well as having a faint purple flush.

Silvery and gold-coloured hebes are valuable for winter colour, adding bright patches to a hebe bed – though of course their colour remains for the rest of the year as well. The blue-grey or silvery hebes will stand out well against those with dark green or purple-tinted foliage. Silvery hebes can really lighten a mass of green plants, showing up particularly well in winter. Gold-toned foliage, as in H. ochracea 'James Stirling', is always welcome on dark days, providing another contrast to deeper foliage colours. The whipcord hebes, which tend to be the ones with yellowish or bronzed foliage, add both colour and texture. Bright green foliage is cheering, too, and the dome shapes of fresh green or emerald-green dwarf hebes look especially good in winter.

Those hebes with shiny or really glossy leaves, including H. decumbens, H. subalpina and H. vernicosa, can also show up well in winter among those with duller or matt leaves. H. odora 'New Zealand Gold', usually a bright, shiny green, can sometimes develop bright golden tips, and these really stand out in winter.

All hebes provide much-needed foliage and stem colour in winter, but those with extra or unusual colour are especially desirable. Many hebes have interesting-coloured stems; some have particularly deeply or brightly coloured young stems that are more noticeable in winter. Examples include:

◆ H. pimeleoides 'Quicksilver': unusual black stems make the silvery leaves more noticeable
◆ H. 'Caledonia': young shoot tips and stems become deep maroon
◆ H. rigidula: yellow-green stems
◆ H. salicifolia: pale yellow-green stems
◆ H. decumbens: deep purple stems that can appear almost black

A hebe bed can look quite striking in winter if planted at least partly with varieties chosen for their interest and colour at this time of year. Choose the hardiest forms for colder areas, and try some of the colourful and variegated but less hardy types in sheltered spots or warmer areas. The following hebes are excellent for winter effect:

◆ For red or pinkish leaf colour, use H. 'Blue Clouds', H. 'Autumn Glory', H. 'Petra's Pink', H. 'Red Edge', H. 'County Park', H. 'Primley Gem'.
◆ Some bright green hebes to include: H. 'Wiri Mist', H. 'White Gem', H. subalpina. Use H. decumbens or H. vernicosa for their really glossy foliage.

As an example of an effective grouping, try the old-gold colouring of the whipcord *H. ochracea* 'James Stirling' together with the dense bright green *H.* 'Wiri Mist' and purple-flushed *H.* 'Autumn Glory'. You will have different leaf sizes and textures as well as the variety of colour.

Shape and scale

It is perfectly possible to plant a hebe bed of any scale, from large to very small. You can have a compact version using dwarf hebes in a tiny front garden, or a large border on a much grander scale.

The type of bed is also immaterial – any shape or style is appropriate, as long as it is in a suitably open spot. You can plant up a square or rectangular bed, perhaps surrounded by paving or low walls; a long border down one side or within the garden; an island bed; an oval or round bed; or an irregularly shaped border in the garden.

Most small beds look best with smaller hebes: choose those that grow to 60cm (2ft) or so in height, with perhaps one or two up to 90cm (3ft) if you want some extra height. If you are planting under a window, whatever scale the border, remember not to plant any that will grow above the sill. You can derive just as much enjoyment from the dwarf hebes, which have a great range of shapes, colours and textures, as well as a variety of flowers.

For larger or wider borders, you have the choice of using taller hebes or a combination of tall, medium and dwarf types. It is more interesting to opt for a mixture of different sizes, shapes and habits, to give a greater variety within the border. The inclusion of some smaller forms allows you to look down at them rather than straight at them, giving a further dimension to the planting. The various heights allow the planting to flow more easily, and

Hebe 'Emerald Green' growing in front of *H.* 'Wiri Mist' and *H.* 'Primley Gem'

some lighter-coloured, smaller-leafed hebes will open up the border rather than presenting you with too much of a solid bulk of large foliage.

Whatever scale you are working on, rounded shapes are comfortable, pleasing and easy on the eye. A group of rounded hebes, such as the smaller dome-shaped types, at the front of the border can be combined with other shapes of hebes around them to create an interesting planting. *H.* 'Emerald Green' or *H.* 'Jasper' are ideal for small beds, while *H. topiaria* or *H.* 'White Gem' grow into wider low mounds if you have more room.

Island beds can be very effective planted up exclusively with hebes. You can walk all around the bed and see all the plants from a relatively close-up position. You can either plant it with low hebes so that you can see over to the opposite side, or you can plant taller hebes in and near the centre, graduating down to smaller forms all around the edge. This need not be symmetrical: you could have a cluster of larger hebes towards one end of the centre, fill the remainder of the centre with medium-sized hebes, and then use dwarf ones around the edge. This achieves a more restful, graduated effect than having tall plants right in the middle. However, the way you plan your bed depends on its position in the garden, where you will be viewing it from, and what effect you want to achieve. Small island beds can be planted in the same way, using hebes in proportion to the scale of the bed.

The planting plans at the end of this chapter are designed to show you some of the effects that can be achieved in a hebe bed.

Examples of hebe plantings

Here are some ideas for hebe combinations to help you get started, considering the points outlined in this chapter.

◆ These three hebes show contrast in shape and foliage, and are all free-flowering with dense racemes. *H.* 'Autumn Glory' has an open, rounded habit, with dark violet flowers late in the season and winter leaf colour; *H.* 'Wiri Mist' has an excellent, distinctive, bushy shape with fresh green leaves and white flowers; *H. albicans* forms a bushy, dense mound with grey-green leaves and pretty white flowers. This is a winning combination for variety of colour, providing grey-green and fresh green leaves together with deep green, red-flushed leaves that become strikingly deeper in colour during winter and spring. The group has a long overall flowering season from early summer to late autumn, with a display of white and dark violet blooms.

Interesting combinations can be put together to give you a wide variety of foliage and plant shape.

◆ For a small bed, you could plant the low-growing *H. carnosula*, with its thick, concave, grey-green leaves, together with the prostrate *H.* 'County Park', whose small grey-green leaves take on pinkish-mauve winter colour, and *H.* 'Christabel', with its bright green whipcord foliage forming a neat dome. The addition of *H.* 'Margret' provides a mound of shiny, bright green foliage, while *H.* 'Wiri Dawn' adds some elegance with its slender, light green leaves.

◆ A larger bed could hold the open, spreading *H. pimeleoides* 'Quicksilver', with tiny silvery leaves, next to *H.* 'Autumn Glory', a rounded bush whose dark green leaves become red-flushed in winter. Add *H.* 'Nicola's Blush', a wide-spreading bushy shrub with mid-green foliage tinged purple and bronze in winter, and the bushy, rounded *H.* 'White Heather', which has shiny leaves. This is also an attractive flowering group, with blue, dark violet, pink and white blooms.

If you plan your hebe bed first, it is easy to work out which hebes will complement or contrast with each other, so that you don't place similar ones together. In this way each hebe will be displayed to its best effect.

For a colourful border, to provide both foliage and flower interest all year round, use a combination of hebes that colour well in winter together with those that have variegated, silvery and fresh green leaves. Choose varieties that flower over as many months of the year as possible, with a wide range of flower colour. A selection for such a border could include:

Hebe	Leaf	Flower	Flowering season
albicans	grey-green	white	early–mid summer
'Alicia Amherst'	glossy dark green	rich violet	midsummer–winter
'Blue Clouds'	deep green/purple	wisteria blue	summer–winter
'Caledonia'	green/maroon	violet	late spring–autumn
'Carnea Variegata'	green/cream/pink	rich rose-pink	summer–autumn
'Kirkii'	glossy green	white	early summer
'Lindsayi'	greyish-green	pale pinkish-lilac	early–mid summer
'Lopen'	bright green/cream	light violet-purple	midsummer–autumn
'Marjorie'	glossy green	light mauve-blue	early summer–autumn
vernicosa	shiny green	pale lilac	mid-spring–summer

The green foliage of *Hebe odora* 'New Zealand Gold' provides a backdrop for the colourful flowers of *H.* 'Heidi'

If you want something a bit different or out of the ordinary, search out the more unusual hebes, particularly the dwarf kinds, which provide such a range of interesting foliage. Mix together whipcords, domes and prostrate or decumbent hebes to provide you with year-round foliage interest, and choose some that flower freely if you want added colour. Look for the following interesting hebes, which really should be more widely grown, as they have a lot to offer the gardener.

- *H.* 'pauciramosa*: upright stems of stiff, shiny leaves
- *H. hectorii*: cord-like yellowish-green branches
- *H. decumbens*: dark stems of shiny leaves
- *H.* 'Edinensis': bright green whipcord hybrid
- *H.* 'Greensleeves': bushy whipcord hybrid, free-flowering

- *H.* 'James Platt': upright dark stems
- *H. rigidula*: neat, well-branched low bush, free-flowering
- *H. cupressoides* 'Golden Dome': dense, golden-bronze whipcord
- *H. vernicosa*: compact, with glossy leaves and attractive flowers
- *H. amplexicaulis* f. *hirta*: distinctive woolly leaves

Add some of the free-flowering low mounds such as *H.* 'Wiri Dawn' and *H.* 'Margret' if you want further flower colour.

When you first plant a hebe bed it will look quite sparse, as you will (hopefully) have left sufficient room around each plant for it to develop and grow. However, by its second year, the plants will be filling out and, if you are correctly pruning them after flowering, they will become bushier, with plenty of new shoots. It is satisfying to watch the hebes developing, noticing their different shapes forming, watching the colours of the leaves change over the seasons and enjoying the flowers when in bloom. If you add a thick bark mulch to the bed after planting, it will look more attractive and help to keep weeds down while the hebes are filling up their allotted spaces.

Hebe bed (part of) *chosen for long flowering season*

Illustrated in early summer

This border planting demonstrates an arrangement of hebes to provide a spread of colour and flowering times. Although the emphasis is on free-flowering types, the foliage is varied enough to add extra interest, particularly over the colder months. These hebes provide colour from mid-spring, all through summer and autumn and into early winter if the weather is mild. Some of the hebes have one flush of flowers, others have two, or a succession of flowers over several months. The bed is very colourful, with flowers of white, pink, pinkish-lilac, light purple-blue, rosy purple, sky-blue and rich violet.

Plants

- ◇1 *Hebe* 'Nicola's Blush'
- ◇2 *Hebe pimeleoides* 'Quicksilver'
- ◇3 *Hebe* 'Amy'
- ◇4 *Hebe* 'Lindsayi'
- ◇5 *Hebe* 'Sapphire'
- ◇6 *Hebe* 'Greensleeves'
- ◇7 *Hebe* 'Pink Paradise'
- ◇8 *Hebe vernicosa*
- ◇9 *Hebe* 'Wiri Charm'
- ◇10 *Hebe* 'Petra's Pink'
- ◇11 *Hebe* 'Wiri Cloud'
- ◇12 *Hebe decumbens*
- ◇13 *Hebe* 'Bowles's Hybrid'
- ◇14 *Hebe* 'Margret'
- ◇15 *Hebe* 'Pewter Dome'
- ◇16 *Hebe* 'Hagley Park'
- ◇17 *Hebe pinguifolia* 'Pagei'

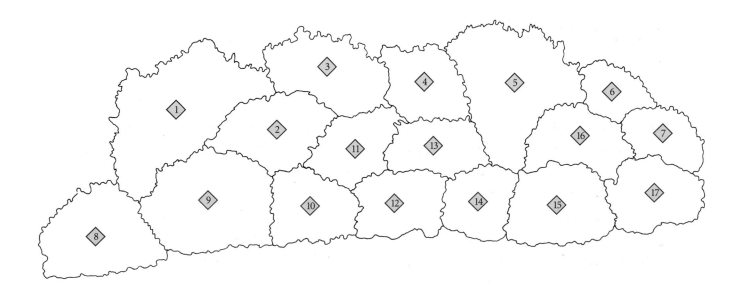

Hebe bed *chosen mainly for foliage interest*

Illustrated in early–mid summer

This bed shows how effective hebes are for providing contrast not only in plant habit, but also in leaf shape, size and colour. The planting includes low mounds, bushy hebes of various sizes, upright and low spreading types. There is a huge range of foliage, with variously coloured whipcords plus woolly, variegated, grey, fresh green and purplish leaves. Many display deepening purplish or maroon colours in winter; *H. loganioides* becomes bronze-tinted. The blooms add touches of white, pale lilac and pink during summer and autumn.

Plants

1. *Hebe hectorii*
2. *Hebe* 'Red Edge'
3. *Hebe* 'Wiri Mist'
4. *Hebe* 'Dazzler'
5. *Hebe bishopiana*
6. *Hebe recurva*
7. *Hebe amplexicaulis* f. *hirta*
8. *Hebe* 'Emerald Green'
9. *Hebe* 'Petra's Pink'
10. *Hebe pinguifolia* 'Pagei'
11. *Hebe pauciramosa*
12. *Hebe* 'Loganioides'

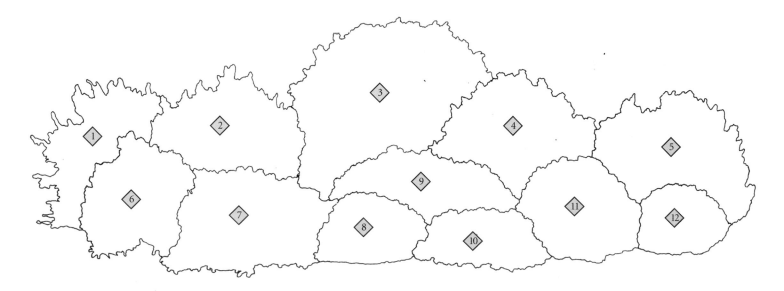

Hebe bed *chosen for all-year-round interest*

Illustrated in early summer

An island bed showing the imaginative use of hebe shapes, foliage texture and colour, flower colour and size, and a spread of flowering season. It looks wonderful all through the year, with its planting of rounded, bushy hebes interspersed with upright forms, together with low and prostrate types around one end. It contains variegated, bright green, deep green, old-gold and grey foliage, with many varieties showing pinkish or purplish tints to provide much-needed colour in winter and early spring. The bed is in flower for much of the year, with colours of pink, rosy purple, violet, wisteria-blue and white, and contains some of the showiest hebes such as 'Blue Clouds', 'Autumn Glory' and 'Caledonia'. (Some of the small hebes are repeated on the other side of the bed, though this is not shown in the illustration; these are indicated in the list by '× 2' alongside.)

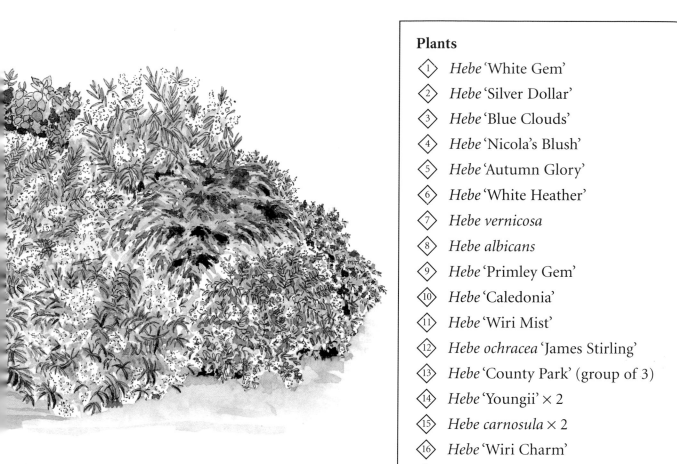

Plants

1. *Hebe* 'White Gem'
2. *Hebe* 'Silver Dollar'
3. *Hebe* 'Blue Clouds'
4. *Hebe* 'Nicola's Blush'
5. *Hebe* 'Autumn Glory'
6. *Hebe* 'White Heather'
7. *Hebe vernicosa*
8. *Hebe albicans*
9. *Hebe* 'Primley Gem'
10. *Hebe* 'Caledonia'
11. *Hebe* 'Wiri Mist'
12. *Hebe ochracea* 'James Stirling'
13. *Hebe* 'County Park' (group of 3)
14. *Hebe* 'Youngii' × 2
15. *Hebe carnosula* × 2
16. *Hebe* 'Wiri Charm'
17. *Hebe rigidula* × 2
18. *Hebe recurva* × 2
19. *Hebe* 'Wiri Dawn'
20. *Hebe decumbens*

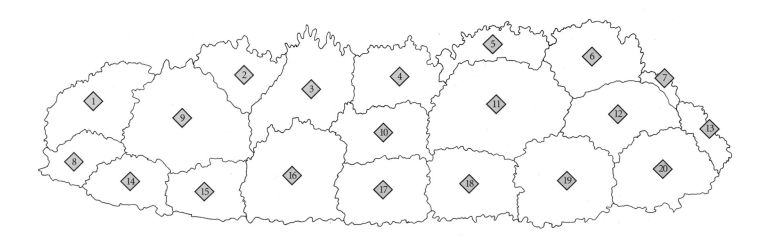

CHAPTER 6

Hebes for containers

Container gardening is increasingly popular – deservedly so, since it is suitable for any size or style of garden. From a single plant in a small pot to a massed planting in a large container, there are endless variations to experiment with. Most containers are movable and can therefore be placed in different positions at various times of the year, depending on where you want them at any particular time.

Suitability of hebes

Hebes are ideal plants to grow in containers, and the dwarf forms in particular are adaptable for all sorts of planting schemes. Some of the medium-sized forms can be used in larger containers, where they will put on a colourful display, but the large hebes are really rather impractical to use as they will quickly outgrow their pots.

A major advantage of hebes is their evergreen foliage, as they can be on display all year, with flowers an added bonus. Non-flowering types are also excellent in pots, often forming good structural shapes. The rounded domes that some hebes grow into are ideal for formal gardens, or for rows or groups of pots; for example, alongside paths, up flights of steps or placed either side of a doorway.

Hebe 'Carnea Variegata' in a colourful container grouping

Use hebes with a long flowering season if you like lots of colour in your pots. Remember, too, that many hebes show deepening leaf flushes and tints over winter, bringing welcome colour in the colder months; in addition, new spring shoots are often purplish, adding a glow to container plantings.

Choose varieties to suit your purpose, whether for foliage, flowers or both, planting either in individual pots or with other plants in a mixed container. We shall be looking at several examples of container planting schemes using hebes.

Types of container

There is a huge range of containers to choose from, made from a variety of materials. Terracotta pots can be obtained either new, or old and already weathered. Glazed earthenware pots are available in bright or muted colours; there are half-depth sizes too, suitable for low-growing hebes. Plastic pots are inexpensive, and can be found in matt terracotta, which is more realistic than the shiny ones. Reconstituted stone planters and tubs are available in greyish or cream colours, and wooden tubs and boxes can be obtained or made in many shapes and sizes.

Make sure there are sufficient drainage holes for the size of the container, and that it is stable. Place crocks in the base to prevent compost blocking the holes.

Individual plants in pots

Dwarf and medium-sized hebes make excellent specimen plants in containers. Choose the container to suit the shape and size of the plant. An ordinary flowerpot shape is fine for most, but the more rounded urn-shaped pots are ideal, as the base is less tapered and therefore holds a greater proportion of compost. Tall, narrow pots can be used for dwarf hebes, particularly for those with a dome-shaped growth habit. Shallower pans and bowls are suitable for slow-growing dwarf types, especially prostrate and mounded forms.

Consider the growth habit and shape of the hebe you choose: those with a neat, compact habit, densely clothed in foliage, are always a good choice, whether flowering or non-flowering. For larger pots, there are bushier hebes, which may have larger leaves more widely spaced on the stems, but can still be relatively compact. Some of the low-growing, spreading hebes also look attractive in pots.

Hebe diosmifolia **is an attractive flowering hebe for a small pot**

Plants for foliage

Some hebes are grown mainly or solely for their foliage, so if you are looking for an evergreen plant for a pot, and aren't particularly concerned about flowers, there are a number of attractive and interesting types to choose from. Some of the whipcords are good value in containers, requiring little or no pruning, and they look bright and fresh all year round. *H.* 'Christabel' and *H.* 'Emerald Green' both form rounded domes of tiny, bright emerald green leaves, and are brilliant if you want a sphere shape in a pot. They can even be trimmed very lightly to create a perfect dome (see Chapter 8). Their bright colour beautifully complements terracotta or earthenware pots, either full- or half-depth. Tall square or round pots also look exceptional with the contrast in shape and proportion. *H. cupressoides* 'Golden Dome' is a stiffly upright whipcord, with a unique golden-bronze colour, ideal for a small pot as it grows very slowly. In larger containers, use *H. ochracea* 'James Stirling' for its stunning old-gold colour and distinctive flat-topped shape. Older plants tend to lose their leaves in the centre, revealing stout, woody branches, which is not unattractive and adds further character.

There are some relatively new hebes with especially attractive foliage, ideal for use in pots. Try *H.* 'Dazzler', with its amazing cream-variegated leaves flushed pinkish-purple; *H.* 'Pink Elephant', with buttery-yellow, green and pink leaves, tinted burgundy in winter; *H.* 'Silver Dollar', whose leaves are variegated green and silver, with red margins and burgundy shoot tips in winter. Any of these will look colourful in a container placed near a door, on a patio or next to a seat. An old favourite is *H.* 'Red Edge', fairly nondescript in summer, but showing off for all it is worth during the colder months, with the grey-green leaves and shoot tips taking on a stunning maroon coloration. For a neat, tidy, all-year-round globe, use *H. topiaria*, with its closely packed, small, grey-green leaves giving the appearance of a clipped bush.

Plants for small pots

Small pots, say 12–20cm (5–8in) in diameter, can easily hold dwarf hebes such as the early-flowering *H.* 'Baby Marie', with neat leaves and pretty pale lilac blooms borne in spring – ideal for a splash of early flower. *H. rigidula*, with its neat upright form and tidy green leaves, then surprises us with its burst of white flowers during late spring to midsummer, completely smothering the top of the plant. The flowers are crowded together very closely on each raceme, giving the effect of a dense white covering.

Plants for flowering

Recommended flowering hebes to use in pots include *H.* 'Bowles's Hybrid', *H.* 'Rosie', *H.* 'Wiri Charm' and *H.* 'Wiri Mist', all of which produce excellent blooms on well-shaped plants. Choose *H.* 'Lindsayi' or *H.* 'White Heather' if you want a slightly taller plant. All of these have good foliage, but it is their flower display that makes them special. Use them among other containers to provide evergreen background foliage for other flowering plants. You can move them, if you wish, to a more prominent position for their flowering display.

Other hebes have both attractive foliage and a good flower display, so are good value on all counts. *H. albicans*, *H.* 'Pimeba', *H. recurva*, *H.* 'Wiri Cloud' and *H. vernicosa*, showing a variety of leaf and flower colour, are all excellent

for containers 20–30cm (8–12in) or so in diameter. For even larger containers, try *H.* 'Nicola's Blush', with its lovely pink and white blooms borne over a very long period, or *H. bishopiana*, which carries many pale lilac flowers on dark-stemmed bushes. Both of these also have deeper leaf tints in winter.

Tender hebes in pots

Some hebes are best confined to a pot so that you can protect them over winter by placing them in a frost-free greenhouse or porch. Move them as soon as there is any danger of frost, and you can enjoy any late flowers that may be produced. Bring them outside again in spring once the worst of the cold weather has passed.

In sheltered areas outside, you can grow *H.* × *franciscana* 'Variegata'; this is often recommended for winter containers, but is not fully hardy, so it is only really suitable in mild areas. Its cream-edged, relatively large, thick leaves are an attractive foil to the violet flowers. You could grow it in a container and keep it under cover for the winter, bringing it out once the frosts are over.

The same can be done for other hebes that may suffer in cold areas, or that aren't reliably hardy. *H.* 'Baby Marie' does well outside in a fairly sheltered spot, and although it usually survives in colder positions, it can suffer badly and take some time to recover. Confined to a pot, you can protect it from the worst of the weather.

H. 'Carnea Variegata' is a rather spectacular variegated hebe, the narrow leaves of light green and creamy-yellow flushed with rosy pink. The long, rich rose-pink flowers are borne during summer and autumn, and it is a favourite with flower arrangers. Unfortunately, it suffers badly in the cold, so grow it in a large pot and give winter protection.

A small whipcord hebe combined with colourful alpines

Hebe chathamica trails down the front of this mixed container

Combinations with other plants

If you want to grow a particular hebe and you know it is not reliably hardy, it really is worth the effort of containerizing it. Stand the pot outside in late spring and summer, either on its own as a focal point, or with other planted containers. You could also position it among plants in the border, where the foliage and flowers will contribute to your summer display.

There are many possibilities for combining hebes with other plants in a container. Your selection can be based on harmonizing or contrasting colours; a variety of interesting foliage; or a long flowering season, choosing plants that will bloom in succession. Try to choose plants that form effective combinations to provide maximum interest. Make sure that all the plants in a given container are compatible, liking the same conditions as hebes – that is, a light position, with a fair amount of sun, and well-drained compost that does not dry out. Use plants of a similar scale to the hebe you have chosen, so that the container planting develops in a balanced way. Combine slow-growing dwarf shrubs, small perennials, alpines and neat grasses with dwarf hebes, and complement medium-sized hebes with perennials and taller grasses, for instance. If you are including more than one shrub, make sure the container is large enough to support them, as they will each need room to develop a decent shape.

Consider the shapes and growth habits of the plants. Many hebes are bushy or dome-shaped, so use upright, spiky and trailing plants with them. Choose plants that have leaves with different shapes, textures and sizes, such as aquilegias, dwarf delphiniums, irises and sedums. Use foliage that is fine and feathery, or rounded and velvety, or needle-like, or really tiny, or succulent and fleshy. All of these will contrast sharply with hebe leaves. Red and purple, golden, silver or variegated leaves will all harmonize or contrast with appropriately selected hebes. Deep red leaves, such as those of *Berberis thunbergii* 'Bagatelle' or *Sedum spurium* 'Purpurteppich', will echo the red leaf margins and midribs of many hebes. The silver foliage of *Santolina*, *Artemisia* or *Achillea* 'Huteri' will add varied textures to grey-leafed hebes and a light touch to plantings of deeper-coloured foliage.

Use the flowers of other plants to blend in or to contrast with those of the hebes. White, pink and lilac will all harmonize gently with similarly coloured hebe blooms, as well as blending with silver or grey foliage. On the other hand, golden or primrose-yellow flowers will contrast beautifully with purple-flowered hebes for a stronger colour scheme. Think of the different flower shapes you can put together. Most hebes have spikes or racemes, which can be short and dense or long and slender, so combine them with the rounded blooms of hardy geraniums, *Cistus* and *Helianthemum*. Foamy or delicate flower heads, such as the myriad little flowers of trailing *Gypsophila repens*, are an effective contrast. The large heads of sedums, each made up of numerous starry flowers, add bright splashes of colour, and there are both alpine and larger perennial varieties, some trailing and others upright. Use pink and white ones with any hebe and yellow ones with purple-flowered or whipcord hebes.

Seasonal additions

For additional colour, incorporate some bulbs when planting your container, or push a few into established containers during autumn. Use dwarf narcissi, irises, muscari and crocuses in small plantings so that they are in scale with the rest of the plants, and restrict the use of taller ones to pots of larger plants. Adding a few colourful pansies, primroses or daisies (*Bellis perennis*) around the rim will also cheer up pots during spring if you don't have much colour at that time. However, you will often find the main plants in the container, particularly hebes and any other evergreens, will provide you with sufficient colour and interest throughout the year. Try planting a hebe instead of a conifer in the centre of a tub, surrounding it with bulbs, pansies and primulas for spring and replacing these with summer bedding plants to follow, using complementary colours.

Narcissus 'Tête-à-tête' provides spring interest in this pot with *Hebe bishopiana*

Examples of successful combinations

This combination of a dwarf hebe with a small lavender and bushy thyme, together with trailing plants, has a soft colour scheme of grey, deep green and variegated leaves with pink and white flowers.

- ◆ *Hebe carnosula*
- ◆ *Thymus* 'Porlock'
- ◆ *Lavandula angustifolia* 'Nana Alba'
- ◆ *Gypsophila repens* 'Rosea'
- ◆ *Hedera helix* 'Adam'

This second planting suggestion includes a mixture of upright, mat-forming and trailing plants with interesting foliage: scale-like whipcord stems, glossy, succulent rosettes and feathery leaves. Golden, green and red foliage creates a background for yellow and blue flowers.

- ◆ *Hebe cupressoides* 'Golden Dome'
- ◆ *Achillea* × *lewisii* 'King Edward'
- ◆ *Sedum oreganum*
- ◆ *Veronica pectinata*

Combinations with other hebes

Similar design principles apply to planting various hebes together in a container. This can provide an excellent year-round feature requiring little maintenance apart from watering, feeding, and pruning where necessary.

In a small pot of 20cm (8in) or so in diameter, you could grow dwarf hebes such as *H.* 'Emerald Green', *H. pinguifolia* 'Pagei' and *H.* 'Baby Marie' for foliage contrast and an early flowering display. A larger container of 25–30cm (10–12in) could hold *H. recurva*, *H.* 'Caledonia' and *H. rigidula*, all compact growers with small leaves, but with a variety of foliage colour and a long flowering season. A 38cm (15in) pot would look splendid with *H. bishopiana*, *H.* 'Wiri Cloud' and *H.* 'Silver Dollar', providing a stunning display of attractive foliage and soft flower colours.

All sorts of combinations can be made, making use of hebes with distinctive characteristics. Use the whipcord hebes for foliage contrast; hebes with long or successive flowering periods to give you lots of blooms; those that take on rich leaf tints in cold weather to provide cheer in winter; and silvery-grey or hardy variegated ones for a lighter leaf colour.

Planting and maintenance

Keep plants in containers regularly watered and fed (see Chapter 9). Prune hebes immediately after flowering, and trim back any perennials or alpines after flowering to tidy them up and encourage new bushy growth. Any other shrubs can be pruned at the appropriate time, and grasses cut back in spring to remove dead leaves and reveal the fresh new growth at the base.

Choice hebes for the alpine house

Some dwarf hebes are rather challenging to grow outside, and benefit from being grown in a pot or pan and kept in a well-ventilated alpine house. This ensures that the worst of the weather is kept at bay, while providing them with sufficient light and air to prosper. These hebes are best grown in well-drained, gritty compost in terracotta pots, plunged into a sand bench. This protects the roots from extremes of temperature and helps prevent either drying out or becoming waterlogged, as the sand is kept moist. Shading can be provided for those that scorch easily in hot sun, particularly those species originating from high altitudes.

As well as more difficult hebes, some of the little ones suitable for troughs, such as *H.* 'Colwall', *H.* 'Tiny Tot' and *H. pimeleoides* var. *minor*, can also be grown in this way.

One challenging species worth trying in an alpine house is *H. tetrasticha*, a semi-whipcord

A choice species, *Hebe cheesemanii*, grows in a terracotta pot in this alpine house

with a distinctly angular appearance to its thin stems. This species dislikes too much sun or heat, so appreciates a lightly shaded position in the alpine house. We have grown it satisfactorily in this way for five years, having raised it from wild-collected seed, and it is now 10cm (4in) high. Another semi-whipcord, *H. cheesemanii,* also does very well in an alpine house, although it can be grown in very gritty soil outside. It reaches 15cm (6in), with grey-green, closely overlapping leaves and white flowers in spring. *H. subsimilis* var. *astonii* is a little yellowish-green whipcord that is difficult to please outside, but thrives more happily in a pot, where its more exacting requirements can be met.

Hebes for sinks and troughs

Some very tiny hebes are perfect for growing in sink or trough gardens, their evergreen foliage adding structure to an alpine planting and their flowers adding colour. These little hebes are perfectly in scale with tiny alpines, and you can use ones with different shapes and a variety of foliage to fit in with whatever miniature landscape you are making. The leaves and flowers are in proportion to the miniature scale of alpine plants, so even those of us with very limited growing space can have a collection of hebes.

An established sink planting with *Hebe raoulii* var. *pentasepala*

Hebe 'Colwall' softens the edge of this sink and provides evergreen structure and interest among alpines

Which hebes to use

Choose prostrate or decumbent forms, such as *H.* 'Colwall', for planting near the edges of your sink, allowing some stems to trail over the sides. These can also be planted at the base of small rocks or tufa pieces, so that their stems gradually creep over some of the rock's surface to soften it.

Little, mounded hebes, such as *H. buchananii* 'Minor' and *H.* 'Tiny Tot', can be used to create hummocks in the sink planting, contrasting with upright or prostrate plants, or to give a different textural quality when combined with the spiky leaves or needle-like foliage of some alpine cushions. Some hebes form spreading mounds,

the centre of the plant building up into a dome, with new stems growing outwards from this. *H. epacridea* is a good example, its stems clothed in stiff, olive-green leaves, with compact heads of white flower spikes.

Other tiny hebes grow into upright, bushy plants, and these can be used to add height to a sink planting. *H. raoulii* var. *pentasepala* is an erect bush 20cm (8in) high, with tiny red-edged leaves and pretty pale lilac flowers opening from pink buds in spring. As with all hebes, the miniature ones include various foliage shapes and colours, with a variety of flowers and flowering periods.

Combining with other plants

You could plant a collection of miniature hebes together in a sink, creating a mini hebe bed, as there is sufficient variety among them for those who are interested enough. Arrange them to show the shapes and foliage colours to advantage, then the little flowers of white, violet or lilac will soften the planting during spring and summer, and deeper leaf tints in winter will add colour during the cold months.

Combined with colourful flowering alpines, these little hebes help to provide year-round interest in a sink. Their evergreen leaves, shrubby habit, and flowers in soft, muted colours, combine effortlessly with most alpines. They will fit easily into a miniature landscape, where the shape may be an important part of the design. They can just as readily be used in a collection of miniature shrubs, or in a mixed planting of alpines. Plant them with tiny *Dianthus*, colourful phloxes, *Geranium dalmaticum*, *Campanula cochleariifolia* 'Elizabeth Oliver', *Alyssum spinosum* 'Roseum' and *Gypsophila repens* 'Fratensis', for a year-round display of silver and green foliage, and flowers of pink, white, magenta, powder-blue and violet.

A miniature shrub planting can be created using two or three tiny hebes together with *Ilex crenata* 'Helleri', *Berberis × stenophylla* 'Corallina Compacta', *Salix serpyllifolia* or *S.* 'Boydii' and *Cotoneaster congestus* 'Nanus'.

Planting a sink

Use a compost mixture of one part by volume each of John Innes No. 2 compost, peat-based compost and grit, adding a layer of broken crocks at the base of all but the shallowest sinks. Shrub and hebe plantings look attractive when finished with a top dressing of very fine bark, but grit should be used when alpines are included in order to provide extra drainage around the necks of the plants. Water well after planting, until the plants are established, and during any prolonged dry spells. Don't allow sinks to dry out; remember, like all containers, they have a limited amount of compost. A sprinkling of a slow-release fertilizer can be applied once or twice a year, in spring and/or autumn.

Hebes to use in sink plantings

Hebe	Height × width		Leaves	Flowers	Flowering season
	cm	in			
H. buchananii 'Minor'	2–4 × 10–15	¾–1½ × 4–6	green, leathery	white	early summer
H. 'Colwall'	5 × 10	2 × 4	green, red edge	violet	early– mid summer
H. epacridea	10 × 20–30	4 × 8–12	stiff, olive-green	white	late spring– early summer
H. 'Jasper'	15–20 × 20	6–8 × 8	glossy, bright green	white	late spring– early summer
H. pimeleoides var. minor	5 × 15	2 × 6	glaucous, grey-green	pale violet	summer– early autumn
H. propinqua	15 × 30	6 x 12	yellow-green	white	summer
H. raoulii var. maccaskillii	15–20 × 15	6–8 × 6	dark green, red edge	lilac	mid–late spring
H. raoulii var. pentasepala	20 × 20	8 × 8	dark green, red edge	pale lilac	mid–late spring
H. 'Tiny Tot'	10 × 10	4 × 4	tiny, green	violet-blue	early– mid summer

Container: hebes only

Illustrated in early summer

30cm (12in) diameter earthenware container

These three hebes share a neat habit with fairly small leaves, but differ in shape and colour and between them have a long flowering season. Golden-green, purple-flushed and glossy green leaves provide a background for the sugar-pink, violet and pale lilac flowers borne over a period from mid-spring to autumn.

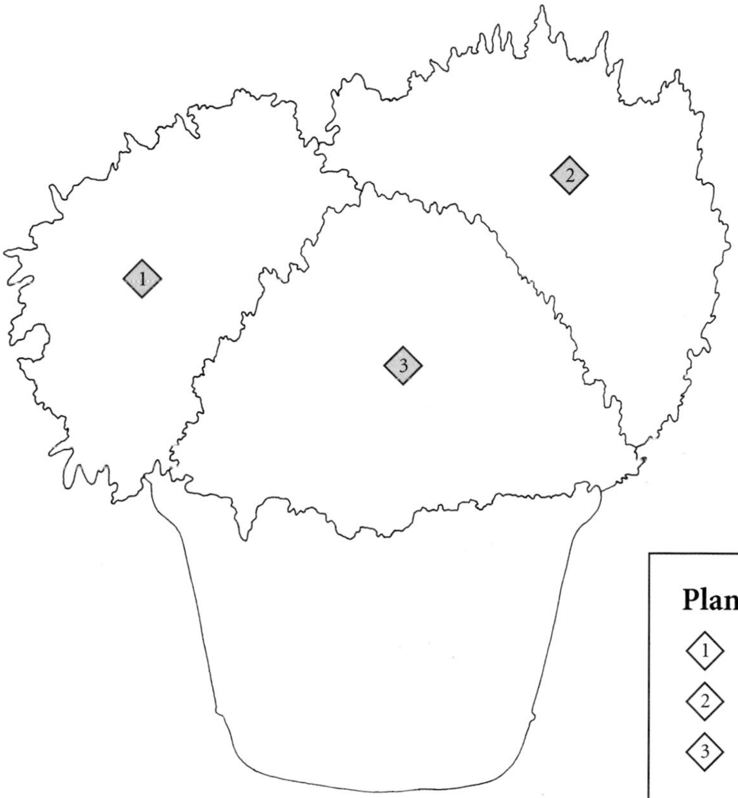

Plants

1. *Hebe* 'Wiri Cloud'
2. *Hebe* 'Caledonia'
3. *Hebe vernicosa*

Alternative

For a container of pink and rose flower shades, replace *H. vernicosa* and *H.* 'Caledonia' with rosy-purple *H.* 'Wiri Charm' and bright pink *H.* 'Rosie'.

Container: hebes in combination with other plants

Illustrated in midsummer

38cm (15in) diameter matt green glazed container

A restful scheme with silver and green variegated foliage and soft grey textured leaves harmonizing with flowers of violet-blue, white, mauve, pale lilac and milky blue.

The hardy fuchsia adds a touch of crimson and magenta, and the hebes have deeper-coloured tips and young leaves in winter. This planting flowers from late spring until late summer. Cut the fuchsia back hard in spring, and trim the remaining plants after flowering.

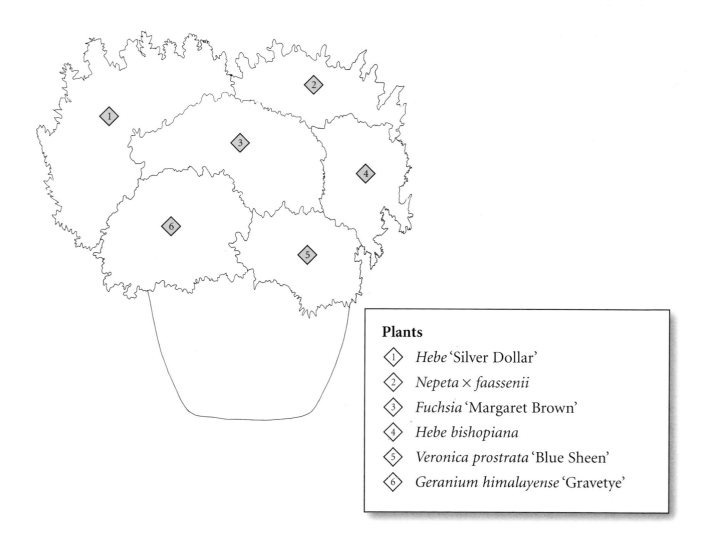

Plants
1. *Hebe* 'Silver Dollar'
2. *Nepeta × faassenii*
3. *Fuchsia* 'Margaret Brown'
4. *Hebe bishopiana*
5. *Veronica prostrata* 'Blue Sheen'
6. *Geranium himalayense* 'Gravetye'

Sink garden

Illustrated in early summer

Stone sink 50 × 35cm (20 × 14in)

A miniature planting with year-round interest, containing five tiny hebes with a range of habit, foliage and flower, together with some compact, colourful alpines. The hebes include an upright bush, creeping or trailing mats and little hummocks, with flowers of white, pale lilac and violet. *Hebe* 'Colwall' provides winter foliage colour. The alpines have contrasting foliage, including iris-like leaves, needle-like hummocks and minute woolly leaves. They provide colour from late spring all through summer, with pink, crimson, blue and white flowers.

Plants

1. *Dianthus* 'Whatfield Wisp'
2. *Geranium dalmaticum*
3. *Phlox douglasii* 'Crackerjack'
4. *Hebe* 'Tiny Tot'
5. *Hebe raoulii* var. *pentasepala*
6. *Sisyrinchium idahoense*
7. *Hebe* 'Colwall'
8. *Thymus serpyllum* 'Minimus'
9. *Hebe buchananii* 'Minor'
10. *Dianthus* 'Berlin Snow'
11. *Hebe pimeleoides* var. *minor*

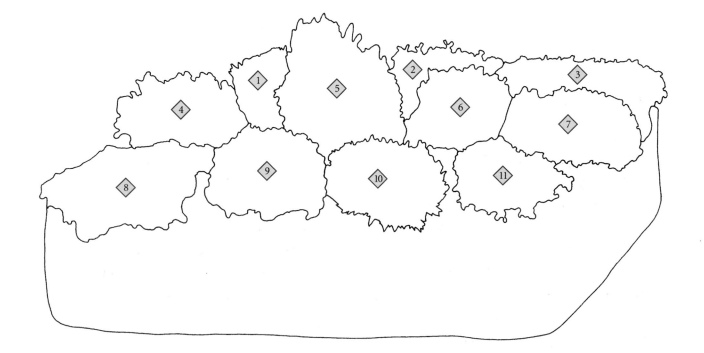

CHAPTER 7

Hebe hedges

Hebe 'White Gem' forms a neat evergreen hedge around a raised vegetable bed

Hedges are used to define both the boundaries of a garden and areas within a garden. They can provide screening, shelter and a background for other plants; lower hedges can define parts of borders or provide an attractive effect in small beds or kitchen gardens. A living hedge can add enormously to the appearance of a garden. Hebe hedges can be utilized in all these ways, subject to the variety chosen and your local climate.

Points to consider

- You need to choose a hebe variety that will withstand the level of wind that you receive in your garden.
- Spacing between plants depends on the vigour and speed of growth of the particular hebe used, and its ultimate size.
- Keep the area around your hedging hebes free of weeds; otherwise the new young plants will suffer from competition for nutrients and water.
- Remove leading shoots and trim frequently in the first two to three years in order to encourage bushiness by allowing the side shoots to grow out. This will form a thicker base to your hedge; otherwise you will have

Hebe rigidula is ideal for a neat, compact hedge

open areas near the base, and all the new growth concentrated nearer the top. Then, depending on the variety used and the type or formality of the hedge, cut annually, either after flowering, or in spring if it is non-flowering.

Types of hedge

Different hebes are suitable for different types of hedge. You may just want an evergreen boundary or background, where flowers are not important, or you may choose a variety that is extremely floriferous over a number of weeks or months, so that it is decorative as well as functional. You may require a tidy, formal hedge or a looser, more informal one.

You can plant hebes in a single row to form a hedge, or stagger them to make a thicker boundary. Strong-growing upright hebes can be used to form a tall, dense hedge. Some of the larger hebes make good informal hedges; their looser, more open habit means they are less successful as formal hedges. However, a well-maintained hebe hedge in full flower is a wonderful sight, and can be extremely attractive.

Hebe 'Jasper' makes a very low, attractive flowering hedge

Dwarf hebes are very successful as formal hedges, because some of them have a naturally dense, compact habit, and respond well to clipping, enabling a tighter, more controlled structure to be achieved. This is particularly true of non-flowering types or those that produce only sparse blooms. Some of the flowering dwarf hebes can make delightful informal low hedges.

Seaside gardens

These have their own problems with regard to hedging, in that plants need to be salt-resistant. As natives of New Zealand, hebes can be very effective in this situation, as they are naturally resistant – particularly those originating from similar coastal regions, where they are exposed to salt-laden winds. However, they are not always completely frost-hardy, so you need to choose suitable varieties; some are better in sheltered, milder areas.

In their native New Zealand, the wild species *H. elliptica* and *H. speciosa* can be found growing by the sea, and are extremely widespread on the coasts of both North and South Islands. A hybrid of these two species, *H.* × *franciscana*, is highly wind-resistant, and can be used as a hedge in coastal regions except in areas that are very cold. A bushy shrub, growing wider than its height, it has large, quite thick leaves that cover the plant densely. The form 'Blue Gem' is popular as a hedging shrub, being both tolerant and attractive, freely producing dense, broad, violet-blue flowers of a good size over a long period.

Hebes to use as hedging

Tall hedges

The following hardy hebes are suitable in gardens for hedges of one metre (3ft 3in) or more.

- *H.* 'Spender's Seedling' is a compact, attractive flowering hedge, producing its flowers over a period of several weeks.
- *H.* 'Edington' is bushy and free-flowering with long violet-purple racemes.
- *H.* 'Mrs Winder' is attractive, with shiny leaves becoming deep reddish-purple in winter.
- *H.* 'Neil's Choice' also has reddish-purple colouring plus rich violet-purple flowers over a long period.
- *H. salicifolia* forms a distinct hedge of long, willowy leaves and pale lilac-blue flowers in long, drooping racemes. It can grow up to 1.8m (6ft), and is suitable particularly for coastal and mild areas, although it is fairly hardy in general.

Medium-sized hedges

These hebes will make hedges 60–90cm (2–3ft) in height.

- *H. odora* 'New Zealand Gold' forms a neat, upright hedge of bright green, shiny leaves.
- *H. subalpina* is bushy, with longer, glossy green leaves and white flowers.
- *H.* 'Nicola's Blush' makes a bushy, informal hedge with masses of pink and white flowers over a very long period.
- *H.* 'Blue Clouds' is showy, with lovely wisteria-blue flowers and foliage that turns deep purple in winter.

- *H.* 'Primley Gem' makes a dense hedge of wavy-edged leaves and pretty mauve-blue flowers.

Dwarf hebe hedges

A dwarf hedge can be defined as one that reaches 15–40cm (6–16in) in height, depending on the variety chosen.

- *H. topiaria* is densely branched, with small, grey-green leaves and a naturally clipped appearance.
- *H. vernicosa* has neat, shiny green leaves and makes a beautiful flowering hedge, with masses of pale lilac flowers.
- *H. rigidula* is a compact, upright and free-flowering species, which forms a very tidy hedge.
- *H.* 'White Gem' is bushy and dense with fresh, light green leaves.

Compact, bushy dwarf hebes with small, densely packed leaves are especially effective when planted as low hedges. They are ideal as alternatives to box (*Buxus*) or cotton lavender (*Santolina*), which are traditionally used for this purpose. In fact, hebes are particularly valuable as replacements for established low box hedges that have been killed or badly affected by disease.

The evergreen foliage remains attractive throughout the year, and you have a choice of bright or dark green, yellow-green or grey-green leaves to harmonize with any colour scheme. The individual plants form neat mounds, which soon merge together to form a close-knit hedge that can be clipped into shape as required once or twice a year.

Ideas for using dwarf hedges

There are several ways of integrating dwarf hebe hedges into the garden:

- ◆ You could plant a hebe hedge around a small bed in order to define its outline and give it a firm boundary. If the bed is planted with low-growing and trailing plants, the hedge will help to contain them and prevent them spilling over onto pathways or grass. In the same way, you could use a low hedge as a division in part of a border, provided it is not likely to be swamped by taller plants.
- ◆ A path or driveway could be enhanced by a dwarf hebe hedge alongside, not only softening the edges but adding foliage and perhaps flower colour to the hard landscaping.
- ◆ Low hedges are ideal in potagers (see below), vegetable or flower beds and knot gardens. Their neat, clipped appearance

enhances rows or blocks of the smaller vegetables, such as salad crops (lettuce, spring onion and radish), or contrasts with upright leeks or onions or the taller, feathery fronds of Florence fennel. Plants grown for cut flowers are also attractive surrounded by a low hedge. The young plants are protected, and a colourful display fills the bed once flowering starts. Use cornflowers, love-in-a-mist, annual chrysanthemums, larkspur and pinks, plus any of your favourites to cut for the house.

A potager is a vegetable garden laid out in a decorative fashion, with beds divided by paths and usually planted up with both vegetables and flowers. These can be laid out in short rows or blocks, arranged aesthetically, using the colours and shapes of plants to contrast or harmonize with their neighbours. Some or all of these beds can be bordered by a dwarf hebe hedge, planting

Hebe rigidula makes a pretty flowering hedge at the end of this driveway

A neat, clipped hedge of *Hebe topiaria* along the side of a vegetable bed

around each bed, or perhaps around the outside edges only. A hedge grown mainly for its foliage and kept neatly clipped looks very attractive, though a free-flowering hebe hedge, such as *H. rigidula* or *H. vernicosa*, adds greatly to the appeal of these more informal beds. Trim immediately after flowering to prevent them flopping and looking untidy.

A potager can be scaled up or down to suit the size of your garden or the amount of space you want to devote to it. The number and size of the beds are your decision, though it is best if you can reach all parts of a single bed from the paths, to avoid treading on it.

Knot gardens are traditionally edged with box (*Buxus*) or cotton lavender (*Santolina*) hedges, and the beds filled either with colourful plants or coloured gravel. The hedges are neatly clipped to give a formal appearance. A similar effect could be achieved with dwarf hebes, and would be particularly useful if an existing box hedge has been devastated by disease. A compact, dense hebe such as *H. topiaria* or *H.* 'White Gem' would be very suitable for a knot garden.

Establishing a hedge

Position

Any hebe hedge must be in an open, sunny position. Shaded or dark areas will cause the plants to grow leggy; leaves will be paler and flowering poor. Any large-leafed hebe should not be planted in an exposed position where strong winds could damage the foliage. Allow sufficient room widthways for the hedge to develop, remembering that the roots will extend further than the foliage and will therefore deplete the soil either side of the hedge.

Soil and preparation

Hebes thrive in well-drained but fairly moisture-retentive soil, disliking dryness at the roots. Don't skimp on preparation – if this is carried out thoroughly, the hebes will establish and grow more successfully and more rapidly.

◆ Clear the area of weeds, taking particular care to remove the roots of perennial weeds.
◆ Add organic matter such as manure, garden compost or leaf mould by spreading a layer 5–8cm (2–3in) thick over the surface, and incorporate it by digging thoroughly. This is particularly beneficial for light, sandy or chalky soils, or for any soil that is likely to be impoverished. Heavy clay soils can have grit added as well, in order to improve aeration. It is advisable to carry out this preparation in early autumn, especially on clay soils, which will subsequently benefit from the action of frost once dug over.
◆ Allow the area to settle before planting.

Selecting plants

We recommend starting a hedge with young, healthy, bushy plants. Larger hebes are generally available in 2–3 litre pots (diameter 16.5–18.5cm, or 6½–7¼in), which gives you a decent-sized plant for a taller hedge that will nevertheless still be young enough to establish quickly and grow away strongly. Dwarf hebes can generally be found in 1 litre (13cm or 5in) pots, or you may be able to purchase young plants in 9cm (3½in) pots from specialist nurseries.

Young plants have plenty of new shoots to grow away strongly once planted, and roots will readily grow away from the root ball into the soil, resulting in more rapid establishment. You can also shape the plants early on in their life to maintain bushiness, and to allow new growth to be produced from the base as well as the tips. However, plants from 1 litre pots will do just as well, provided they are still growing strongly and are not root-bound in their pots. Older, larger specimens are more difficult to trim into a good shape and are less likely to 'knit' together successfully.

In all cases, choose good, healthy-looking specimens that have plenty of new, fresh shoots all round the plant, and that do not have a lot of bare stem near the base.

Planting distances

The spacing of individual plants for a hebe hedge depends on the variety, the eventual height and spread of the hedge, and how quickly you want a dense or closely knitted hedge.

Hebes used for screening or tall hedges, generally those growing to 1–1.5m (3ft 3in–4ft 6in) or so, can be planted at a distance of 60–80cm (2ft–2ft 8in) apart. Bushy hebes can be planted further apart than more erect forms. You need not allow the same amount of space for each plant to develop widthways as you would for a single specimen shrub, as the idea is for the plants to merge together. However, they still need some room to grow out, so don't be tempted to squash them too closely together. They will look too far apart to start with, when newly planted, but you will be surprised at how quickly they fill in the gaps.

Medium-sized hedges, using hebes up to 60–90cm (2–3ft) in height, can be planted 30–45cm (12–18in) apart, again allowing for the natural bushiness or more upright growth of

A newly planted hedge of *Hebe* 'White Gem' around a potager bed

the variety used. Dwarf hebes, used for low hedges 20–40cm (8–16in) high, are planted 20–30cm (8–12in) apart. These denser, more compact hebes are normally used to form a neat, clipped hedge, so can be planted closely together.

Planting and establishment

For a straight run of hedge, use a line to determine the length and to make sure you plant accurately. A piece of string or twine between two posts or canes is ideal.

Make sure the compost in the pot is moist before planting; soak it in a bucket of water beforehand if necessary. Dig a hole in the soil larger than the root ball, then tip the plant carefully out of the pot and place in the hole, making sure the top of the compost is more or less level with the surface of the soil. Fill in with soil, firming gently, adding a small amount of slow-release general fertilizer at the same time, if you have not done this in your initial soil preparation. Measure the distance to the next planting hole, and repeat with the remaining plants. Then water all the plants in thoroughly. Adding bark mulch around the plants helps to keep moisture in the soil, aiding establishment, and reduces maintenance by helping to keep down weed growth.

Planting is best carried out between late spring and autumn, allowing plenty of time for the roots to grow out and the plants to establish while the soil is warm. Although containerized plants can be put in at any time of year, it is best to avoid planting young hebes during the winter, particularly if your soil lies wet at this time of year.

Maintaining a hedge

Provided you have used healthy plants to begin with and prepared the soil adequately, your hedge should grow away and produce fresh new growth

fairly quickly. The plants need time to get their roots down into the soil, and you need to ensure that they have no chance of drying out at this critical time. On the other hand, you don't need to soak them every day so that they become waterlogged. Give them a thorough watering when newly planted and then water every two to four days, depending on the weather. If it is hot and sunny, or there is a drying wind, they will require more water more often than if it is still and overcast. More frequent watering will be needed if your soil is light than if you have clay soil.

Once established, the roots should be deep enough to find sufficient water even in dry spells. Any hedges used in potagers and vegetable beds will get watered anyway when you are watering your crops. Apply a general fertilizer around the base of your hedge once a year, in spring, as the closely spaced plants will soon deplete the soil of nutrients.

Clipping, trimming and pruning

You can lightly trim your hedge the first year, even though the plants will still be quite small. You may feel you would rather let the plants grow to a decent height first, but this means they grow upwards rather than being encouraged to shoot out. We would always recommend at least a light trim in the early stages, to encourage new bushy growth both near the base and from the sides, as well as upwards growth. Use secateurs to trim lightly along the top and around the sides of each plant.

Lightly trimming a hedge of *Hebe* 'White Gem' to create an informal shape

Hebe hedges can be also be clipped hard into more formal shapes

The hedge can then be clipped or pruned each year, once or twice depending on the size of hedge and the degree of formality you want to achieve. Use secateurs on young and small hedges, and shears or a hedge trimmer for established hedges. A hedge trimmer can also be used with care on an established dwarf hedge.

Non-flowering hedges are best trimmed or pruned in spring, or in late spring and then again in late summer if you are aiming for a more tightly controlled hedge. Flowering hebe hedges must be pruned immediately after flowering, both to improve the shape and to prevent woody, leggy growth. Remove any damaged or dead stems at the same time as pruning, cutting them out completely with secateurs. Hedges that are frequently clipped will benefit from a good

On established hedges, clipping can be carried out using a hedge trimmer

An established hedge regrowing well after an earlier hard trim

watering and a liquid feed, using a proprietary liquid fertilizer, once they have been clipped, to encourage new growth.

Renovating a hedge

A neglected hedge responds most readily to renovation in spring, just as new growth begins. You may have inherited a hebe hedge that you want to retain, but if it has not been pruned for a long time, it may be too tall, too wide or in poor shape. Cut back to a point just below the height you would like the hedge to be, provided some growing shoots still remain. If the hedge is excessively woody and leggy, cut back to a height that still leaves some live growth, then repeat the following year, cutting a little lower once more shoots have grown out. Use a saw, shears or secateurs, depending on the size of the hedge. You can reduce excessive width by cutting back one side hard the first year, and the other side the second year, to give the hedge a chance to recover.

After any hard pruning or cutting back, help the hedge to grow and recover by feeding and mulching generously. Use a slow-release fertilizer, or blood, fish and bone, or bone meal. Apply according to the manufacturer's instructions, and follow with a thorough watering. A dressing of any of these fertilizers can be applied once a year in spring, to encourage healthy growth and strong root development.

CHAPTER 8

Training hebes: Topiary and standards

Topiary

Topiary involves the shaping of plants by clipping them into specific shapes or forms. This art, often imitative or imaginative, has long been applied to box (*Buxus*), which is ideally suited, as its leaves are small and closely packed together.

The idea of using dwarf hebes for simple topiary occurred to us after we had started clipping certain hebes closely in order to form neat, low hedging. Hebes with dense growth and small, neat leaves are perfect candidates for clipping into different shapes. Another important consideration is that they are evergreen.

Although topiary is thought of as an art form, shrouded in mystery and requiring many hours meticulously forming intricate shapes, all gardeners can successfully attempt it. You simply need sharp tools, the right plants and some confidence. It does not take long to either form or maintain a simple basic shape such as a sphere or a cone. In this chapter we shall be looking at ways of creating simple topiary shapes from dwarf hebes, which can be used in a variety of ways in the garden.

An established standard of *Hebe rigidula* in full flower

Recommended hebes to use

For creating small-scale shapes:

◆ *H.* 'Jasper': neat dome with tiny, bright green leaves.

For larger topiary shapes:

◆ *H. rakaiensis*: a dense, bright green mound.
◆ *H. topiaria*: even its name suggests its suitability. A naturally compact and neat grower, though it can grow quite wide as a specimen plant.
◆ *H.* 'White Gem': fresh green and bushy.

Characteristics required for topiary

Plants ideally need to have dense growth with short, much-branched stems, so that they do not open out too much, exposing large gaps. If they are slow-growing, less frequent trimming will be required, but you can still have a decent-sized bush by choosing the right variety. For example, *H.* 'Jasper' will stay very small, whereas *H. topiaria* can eventually become quite wide, up to 60cm (2ft), and can therefore be clipped into more definite shapes.

It is important to have varieties with small, neat, closely packed leaves. Not only do they clothe the stems more effectively, and therefore create a much denser structure, but clipping and trimming will cause less damage to the leaves, and will be less noticeable than on large leaves.

You can start with a young plant, say 12–18 months old, and clip it into shape as it grows; or, in some cases, you can shape an already established hebe.

Types of shape

Geometric shapes are both pleasing and relatively easy to achieve, and can be readily adjusted to a small scale.

Sphere

The easiest and simplest shape to achieve is a sphere or ball, as this closely resembles the natural dome shape of suitable hebes, and just requires clipping into a more definite rounded shape. If you have a young plant, use sharp scissors or a pair of fine secateurs to cut carefully all around the plant, trimming the ends of the shoots. Work methodically, creating as round a sphere as possible. Turn the pot round frequently, or move around the plant if it is in the ground, and trim just a little at a time. Shape the plant in at its base to form a rounded structure. You will probably find you need to trim more from the base and top to start with than from the sides. It is easiest to start by first trimming horizontally around the plant to determine its circumference. You can then curve the top and base more accurately so that the ball is symmetrical.

Brush off loose pieces of stem and leaf frequently as you work, so that you can clearly see how you are progressing. Assess continually to make sure you are keeping the shape symmetrical. Don't worry if there are a few gaps to start with, as these will fill in with new growth. Retrim once or twice a year in late spring or early summer.

Cone or pyramid

You will need a hebe with a strong leader shoot (that is, a strong, upright main shoot), as the centre of the

To create a sphere:
1 Trim horizontally around the plant to determine its circumference

2 Curve the top and base more accurately to create a symmetrical sphere

shape needs to be taller than the rest. Clip downwards from the centre point of the plant, imagining a central vertical line running down it, to make a downward strip. Repeat all the way around the plant.

Ball on a stem

This involves allowing a short stem to develop, which is eventually clear of leaves, with a rounded shape on top of it.

Flat, low shape

Plant several young hebes close together and trim to form and maintain a low, flat shape, for example a square or rectangle. This is effective among paving or for making a feature in gravel.

You will find that a pleasing effect can be achieved relatively quickly. Use a young, healthy hebe, which is growing well and already has an even shape. If you are buying a hebe to start with, choose one with fairly symmetrical growth all round, that has fresh, healthy-looking leaves. If you are growing your own from cuttings, keep them trimmed well in the young stages to encourage them to bush out from the start.

Keep them lightly trimmed while growing on until large enough to shape.

To maintain a really sharp outline, you need to trim at least twice a year. However, new growth gives a charming, softened effect, and an effective shape can be maintained by a yearly trim. Once established, clip back to old growth, or the shape of your plant will gradually expand.

Tools

Hand shears allow methodical trimming, removing a little at a time. It is easy to remove too much growth and spoil the shape, so trim a little and then go round the plant again if necessary. Make sure your shears are kept sharp, as blunt blades will pull on the leaves and stems and cause unnecessary damage and tearing. Use secateurs if you are training hebes with large leaves, and for initial trimming on young or small plants, as you can control the cutting more accurately. Precision mini-shears or scissors are excellent for really accurate topiary, particularly on small plants and for keeping a sharp outline.

To create a low, flat shape:
1 Plant several young hebes close together

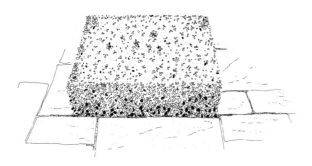

2 As they grow and knit together, trim to form a low, flat shape such as a square or rectangle. This is very effective in paving or gravel

Maintenance

◆ Keep plants weed-free, whether in pots or in the ground.

◆ Water them in dry spells, particularly in the case of newly planted specimens and those in containers.

◆ Feed once a year with a slow-release fertilizer.

◆ Once established, trim regularly, either once or twice a year, to maintain shape.

Incorporating hebe topiary in the garden

Hebe topiary can be effective even in a small garden. You could use a single specimen in a container as a focal point, or place it outside a door. A pair either side of a door gives a more formal look, planted in smart containers or wooden boxes. Simple geometric shapes used in the garden can add a soothing serenity, with rounded shapes in particular giving a softening effect to a border or other feature.

Hebe topiary shapes in containers can add a restful, calm element to your patio or to an arrangement of containers with flowering plants. Use an individual specimen to form a focal point on a small scale – this can be effective on a patio or terrace, or placed on a gravel garden, or among troughs and other small containers. Place several hebe topiary specimens together, either having the same or different shapes, to emphasize an area, or place them alongside a path or up a flight of steps.

A formal effect can be achieved by placing neatly clipped, geometric topiary shapes in particular places. They are very effective used on paving or gravel, either by planting in a symmetrical or ordered way, or by using specimens in containers.

Alternatively, you can introduce an element of fun into your garden by using either geometric or more unusual shapes, placing specimens in borders, on patios or wherever you wish.

Another way of introducing topiary is to incorporate clipped specimens among dwarf hebe hedges. We have already seen, in the previous chapter, how these low hedges can be successfully used in potagers, or for edging borders or small beds. Try clipping a specimen into a sphere or cone at each corner, or on opposite corners, using either the same hebe as that used for the hedge, or a different variety to give a contrast in leaf colour. The same can be done in knot gardens, using clipped hebes instead of the traditional box (*Buxus*).

Hebes used for topiary can be planted in the ground or in containers. In the ground, plant a young specimen and clip into shape as it grows. You will need to move around the plant when clipping, viewing from all angles to make sure you achieve an even shape.

Container-grown hebes are best potted in compost made up of equal volumes of peat-based compost and John Innes No. 2 (soil-based) compost, using a pot suited to the size of the plant. You can subsequently pot on into a larger size as the plant grows. Make sure the compost is never allowed to dry out, and incorporate a slow-release fertilizer, adding a small amount each year to the surface of the compost. Stand the container up on a table or bench when you clip the hebe, as it is much easier to view at or near eye level. You can turn the container regularly as well, to ensure even clipping and shaping.

There is an enormous range of containers to choose from. The container you use should have adequate drainage, and ideally the neck should be wider than or as wide as the base, to ensure easy removal of the root ball when you need to repot.

Terracotta pots look wonderful with clipped specimens in them, and will weather attractively with age, but they do require more frequent watering because of their porosity. Earthenware and glazed pots are very suitable, and are available in a wide range of sizes and colours. Realistic-looking terracotta-coloured plastic pots are ideal if you want more lightweight containers that you can move easily.

Standards

A standard is a plant trained on a clear single stem – that is, a length of stem from which all leaves and lower branches are removed. The head is then shaped, most commonly into a sphere or dome, though cubes and cones are also possible.

Some hebes can form very effective standards. We have experimented with both dwarf and medium-sized hebes. The extra height afforded by having a shape on top of a stem can be useful to add emphasis to a container planting or the corner of a bed, and can add an extra dimension to a low planting. Small-leafed hebes form denser heads, while those with larger leaves form more open heads.

We have successfully trained standards using *Hebe rigidula* and *H.* 'Amy', each of which forms a very different specimen. *H. rigidula* has neat, green leaves, forming a compact head, and is exceptionally pretty when smothered in white flowers. Specimens have reached 40cm (16in) in height, on a stem 25cm (10in) high. *H.* 'Amy' has much larger leaves, with an overall purple colour, forming a more open head on a much thicker stem, with rich purple-violet flowers appearing from midsummer. Shoots are more upright-growing, so it forms a less spherical shape, but makes an impressive feature.

Method of training

To train a standard, you need a young, healthy hebe with a strong leader shoot, as upright as possible.

To encourage the development of a strong main stem, train the standard by gradually

Select a young, healthy hebe with a strong leader shoot (this is *Hebe rigidula*)

Using sharp secateurs, remove the lower branches from the main stem

The young hebe after the first stage of trimming

Tie the stem to a cane to provide additional support while the stem strengthens

removing the lower branches in stages over one or two whole growing seasons. This allows them to contribute to the growth of the plant before their removal. Continue to remove lower branches until the desired length of clear stem is achieved. During this period, leave the head of the plant untrimmed until the leader reaches the desired height. Then pinch out the leading shoot and lightly trim the rest of the shoots to encourage them to branch out and thicken up the head of your young standard. You will probably not have a completely spherical shape yet, but as the plant matures it will become denser. Remove any lower shoots on the stem.

In subsequent years, trim in early and late summer to maintain a spherical head. Turn the plant as you work, removing a little growth at a time. Remove any leaves from the main stem and suckers from ground level as soon as they arise.

Staking

It is best to use a cane or stake when training a new standard, to ensure it grows upright and straight; leave it in until the stem is strong and mature enough to do without one. Put the cane in the pot as close to the stem as possible, avoiding excessive damage to the roots, and attach to the stem using plastic-coated wire ties, twine or plant rings. You need to stake firmly but not too tightly. As the plant grows and its stem thickens, check that the ties are not too tight, and loosen when necessary. Do not let them dig into the stem at any stage, or you will spoil the appearance of it.

Using standards in the garden

Standard hebes are excellent in containers or tubs, either side of a door or at the end of a path. You can plant them in the centre of a container or

On established standards, trim the head back by about one third after flowering

The finished, neatly trimmed standard

wooden box, adding low flowering plants at the base: try long-flowering perennials, or a seasonal change of plants. Keep well watered and fed, as with hebe topiary, trimming each summer to keep a good shape to the head. Make sure the container suits the height and size of the plant.

Use your standard hebe as a centrepiece in a small bed of low-growing plants or in a potager;

as a focal point on the patio, alongside paths or a door; or to give height to a collection of container plants. Make sure you don't hide the stem behind other plants, though, or the effect of all your hard work and skill will be lost.

Keep it in a sunny position, in a spot that is not too exposed, and where the wind is not likely to topple the plant.

CHAPTER 9

Cultivation

Position and soil

Hebes are tolerant of a wide range of soils and planting positions, the ideal being an open, sunny position in a soil that never dries out completely. They can be grown in north-facing borders, provided they get plenty of light and are not in deep shade. They will not, however, succeed under trees, where it is dark and the soil is very dry. Plants grown in too much shade will lose their foliage colour, become drawn and leggy, and may not produce any flowers.

Hebes will grow in most garden soils, preferring a neutral to slightly alkaline soil, though some species will grow in peaty or acid soils. Hebes will thrive in heavy clay soils provided they do not become waterlogged in winter. Heavy soil is best improved prior to planting by incorporating well-rotted compost. The addition of fine grit will help to open out the structure and allow the soil to drain more freely in winter.

Hebes produce a mass of fibrous roots, which allows them to grow well in shallow soils, particularly over chalk. Most hebes will also grow well in light, sandy soils, although these are best improved by the addition of organic matter where possible. Whipcord hebes are an exception: many of these will not thrive in light soils, becoming brown and dried out in the late summer and early autumn.

Pinch out the tips of shoots to encourage bushy growth

Planting

Hebes will grow away quickly once planted; the best results are usually obtained by planting young but well-rooted plants. As a guide, choose plants in pots no larger than 3 litres (18.5cm or 7¼in), and then only when they look fresh and healthy. Larger specimen plants may look good when planted, but they seldom develop well and may not thrive in subsequent years.

Hebes produce a dense system of fibrous roots, which very quickly fill a pot and create the impression of an old pot-bound plant. The best indication of the age of a plant is to look at the base of the plant itself, which should look fresh, without too many dead or brown lower leaves.

Hebes should be planted in the same way as any other container-grown plant:

1 Ensure the compost is moist before planting. If it has become dry, soak the root ball in a bucket of water for at least one hour before planting.
2 Dig a hole at least twice the diameter of the pot and slightly deeper than required. Loosen the bottom of the hole and the surrounding soil.
3 Mix a small amount of bone meal into the base of the hole.

4 Loosen the roots before planting by gently teasing them out at the base. If the root ball is firm, stimulate new root growth by cutting a shallow cross into the base of the root ball.

5 Place the hebe into the hole and backfill with soil, firming the soil gently around the root ball.

6 Water the hebe in well to settle the soil around the roots.

7 Pinch out the tips of the shoots to encourage bushy growth.

8 Newly planted hebes should be kept moist by regular watering until they become established.

Planting in a container

To plant a hebe in a container, follow the steps above, using a compost mixture of one part peat-based compost to one part soil-based John Innes No. 2 compost. Container-grown hebes need to be 'potted on' or repotted every one or two years. The fibrous root system rapidly fills a container and, if left, the roots will become so dense that the compost will not be able to hold moisture. The best time for replanting is in the early spring. If you do not want to increase the size of the pot, lift the plant from its pot in early spring and carefully trim the roots all round by about one third, removing some of the old compost at the same time. You can then replant in the same pot using the compost mixture mentioned earlier.

Watering and feeding

Hebes are generally tolerant of fairly dry conditions once they are established, though the majority thrive better in well-drained but retentive soil. They all benefit from regular watering when first planted. If the soil has been improved as suggested earlier, then after three to four months they will only need watering in severely dry conditions or on very sandy soils.

Hebes in containers need regular, thorough watering, especially on hot and windy days. In the winter they will benefit from having their pots raised off the ground on a tile or a piece of wood to allow excess water to drain away.

Hebes in the ground will benefit from a light dressing of a balanced fertilizer such as Growmore or blood, fish and bone in early spring. Hebes have shallow roots, and care should be taken to spread the fertilizer evenly around the base of the plant to prevent scorching of the roots.

A large hebe which has just been moved will benefit from a liquid feed with a balanced fertilizer for a month or two until the roots develop into the surrounding soil. Heavily pruned hebes such as hedges or standards will also benefit from a liquid feed after trimming to help speed up regrowth.

Container-grown hebes must be fed regularly, the frequency depending on the fertilizer used. Slow-release fertilizers need only to be used once or twice a year, but liquid feeds should be applied regularly throughout the spring and summer.

Pruning hebes

If left to develop unpruned, hebes will often grow into quite neat and tidy bushes. This has led to the common misconception that they do not need pruning. The problems usually arise as the plants grow older, and they gradually become leggy and bare at the base. The larger hybrid hebes, in particular, can rapidly outgrow their allotted space if left unchecked. Once this stage is reached it is very difficult to bring them back under control.

An established bush of *Hebe* 'Nicola's Blush' before pruning

Prune back by about one third

Hebes should be pruned regularly from when they are young. In their early years the new growth should be trimmed lightly after flowering each year. As the plant reaches the desired size it should be cut back hard, removing most but not all of the current year's growth. As a general guide, cut back by about one third. This will help to maintain its size and keep the plant neat and full of leaf at the base.

Late-flowering hebes such as *H.* 'Nicola's Blush' or *H.* 'Autumn Glory' should be pruned in the early spring. Pruning in late autumn can encourage soft, easily damaged growth over winter. Non-flowering hebes (apart from whipcords) are best trimmed in the early spring, again starting with a light trim on young plants and removing more as they reach the desired size.

Hebes do not respond reliably to drastic pruning into old wood. Sometimes they will regrow well, but in many cases the growth is either very weak or non-existent. Old, leggy plants are

The pruned bush will soon green up and produce new shoots again

usually best replaced with new plants. If you have to try to regenerate the plant, it is best done in stages, cutting one third of the plant hard back each year and just cutting back the new growth on the rest of the plant.

A plant of *Hebe* 'Autumn Glory' that has been left untrimmed and has become leggy

Prune out old, leggy shoots down to the base

The fresh growth at the base will soon grow away, and should then be trimmed regularly to prevent legginess

In addition to a general prune each year, it is sometimes necessary to remove damaged branches, particularly after a severe winter. This should be done in the early spring or as soon as the damage occurs, cutting below the damaged areas to encourage regrowth.

The whipcord hebes are the exception to these pruning rules. Many of these do not respond well to pruning, particularly the more rigid types such as *H. ochracea* 'James Stirling'. Some of the softer whipcord hybrids such as *H.* 'Emerald Green' will benefit from light trimming when they are young.

As with the other types, dead or damaged branches should be cut out at their bases as soon as possible. *H. ochracea* 'James Stirling' and similar types can if necessary be reduced in size by removing whole branches at the base, although care should be taken to avoid leaving an unevenly shaped plant.

Remove a shoot with four to five pairs of leaves, using sharp secateurs

Propagation

Cuttings

Hebes will root readily from cuttings at most times of the year. In our experience, the best time for planned propagation is in the late summer. Cuttings taken at this time will root over winter if left uncovered in a greenhouse or cold frame. They will root readily during the spring and early summer, but a great deal of care is needed to prevent them getting too hot, as they will scorch very quickly.

Cuttings should be taken from the current year's growth just as it begins to harden at its base, following these steps:

1. Using sharp secateurs, cut shoots four to five pairs of leaves long from the tips of the plant, cutting between pairs of leaves.
2. Trim the lower leaves from the stem to give enough clear stem to support the cutting when it is inserted into the compost. With the whipcord types the minute leaves should be left on the stem, as they are too small to remove without causing severe damage.
3. Dip the end of each cutting into a proprietary rooting hormone containing a fungicide. As well as speeding up the rooting process, the added fungicide helps to prevent rotting at the base of the stem.

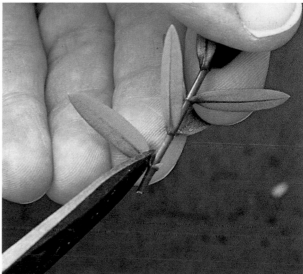

Remove lower leaves from the cutting

Dip the base of the cutting in rooting hormone

Insert the cutting in a pot of cutting compost

Place the pot of cuttings in a cold frame and water in thoroughly

4 Using compost made up of one part peat to one part fine perlite, insert the cuttings so that the lowest pair of leaves is just above the compost. If you only need a small number of cuttings, use clean 9cm (3½in) pots, inserting about five cuttings into each pot. For large numbers, multi-celled propagation trays are ideal: these keep the roots of individual cuttings separate, making them much easier to handle when they are ready to pot up. Water the cuttings in thoroughly.

5 The cuttings should be placed in a greenhouse or cold frame and shaded from direct sunlight. Cuttings taken in late summer do not need to be covered with polythene or placed in an enclosed propagator within the greenhouse or cold frame.

6 Leave the cuttings to root over the winter, and by early spring they will have developed strong, healthy root systems. Placing the cuttings on a heated bed can speed up rooting, but they should not be covered, as this will encourage downy mildew. While they are rooting, the cutting compost should be kept moist but not wet. Remove any dead leaves as they fall, to prevent the spread of mould.

7 In early spring, pot the cuttings into individual 9cm (3½in) pots using a good-quality potting compost. Leave them to grow on in a well-ventilated greenhouse or cold frame until early summer. By this time they will have developed a good root system and will be ready for planting out into their final positions.

Using this system we normally achieve between 90 and 100 per cent rooting for most hebe species and varieties except the whipcord types. In our experience these can be slow to root, and we sometimes get rooting percentages as low as 30 to 40. We have found that simply inserting more cuttings is the easiest solution.

Seeds

Hebes can be grown quite easily from seed, and established plants will often seed around freely in the garden. However, hebes cross-pollinate freely with each other, and as a result the seedlings produced will show considerable variation. This uncontrolled crossing has resulted in many of the best hybrids, such as *H.* 'Nicola's Blush' and *H.* 'Caledonia'. The only hebes that will come true from seed are the species, and then only if they are grown in isolation from other hebe species.

If you want to experiment with seeds, collect them from the plant as soon as they are ripe and then sow them immediately. They should be sown onto a mixture of equal parts of peat-based compost and John Innes No. 2 compost. Cover the seeds with a layer of fine grit and place them out of the sun in an unheated greenhouse or cold frame. Seeds sown in the autumn should have germinated by the following spring.

Once the seeds are large enough to handle, pot them on into 9cm (3½in) pots and grow them on as described for cuttings. The seedlings you produce may be very variable in size and colour – but with luck you may produce a successor to 'Nicola's Blush'!

Troubleshooting

Drought

Hebes are generally tolerant of fairly dry conditions once they are well established. In prolonged dry spells on thin soils or in containers, the first sign of distress is usually a dulling of the foliage, which then becomes thin and papery. At this stage they will usually recover if watered thoroughly – with container plants, plunging the pot in a container of water is the best way to make sure that the compost is thoroughly re-wetted.

A common symptom of chronic drought is yellowing of the lower leaves. This will happen gradually with most hebes as the old leaves die off; but if the plant is suffering from drought stress, the yellowing will often progress well up the plant and affect even the current year's growth. When these symptoms occur, watering should be increased and the compost or soil kept moist at all times, particularly during hot summer days. Little can be done about the damage to the plant once the symptoms are visible, except to trim back the plant to tidy the growth and encourage new shoots to develop. To prevent the problem recurring, container plants should be repotted as already described. For plants in the soil, digging in well-rotted compost around the plant will help to retain moisture and encourage rapid regrowth.

Yellowing of lower leaves of *Hebe albicans* due to drought

Yellowing of shoot tips on the whipcord hybrid *Hebe* 'Emerald Green', due to waterlogging

Frost damage on leaves of *Hebe* 'Nicola's Blush'

Whipcord hebes are particularly prone to drought; while they will show little signs of short-term stress, they are very susceptible to summer drought, the symptoms of which often do not appear until well into the autumn or winter. For this reason they are best not planted on very thin, sandy soils where summer droughts are a problem. On the other hand, waterlogging in winter can cause yellowing of the shoot tips, but they usually grow away from this in spring.

Wind scorch

Wind scorch can be a problem with some hebes, the worst damage often occurring in early spring, when cold winds can damage the soft new growth. The effects are usually seen as a browning of the tips of new growth on the windward side of the plant, although small plants may be damaged all over.

Unless the damage is very severe, plants will usually grow away once the weather improves; a light trim to remove the brown tips is all the treatment that is required.

Frost damage

Frosts of −5°C (23°F) or below will kill or severely damage the tender hybrids, but most hebes will survive all but the coldest frosts. Some of the larger-leafed hybrids such as *H.* × *franciscana* 'Variegata' will be defoliated by moderate frost but will generally shoot again once the weather warms up. These hebes are best cut back to new shoots once growth restarts, to retain a neat, compact shape.

In severe conditions even the hardiest hebes may show some browning on the leaf edges and shoot tips similar to that caused by wind scorch. Again, this is best trimmed off in the early spring once the weather begins to improve, and the plant will then grow away rapidly.

Sparse flowers are typical of some hebes, such as *Hebe topiaria*

Poor flowering

Irregular or sparse flowering is usually a characteristic of the particular species or hybrid, rather than a cultural problem. Some hybrids, such as *H*. 'White Gem', will flower freely one year and then have just one or two for the next few years. Some species, such as *H. topiaria*, never flower freely, just having small clusters of flowers each year. Others, such as *H*. 'Red Edge' and *H*. 'Mrs Winder', rarely flower well, even though they are frequently sold as flowering hebes.

Hebes need an open, well-lit position to flower well, and the most common cultural reason for lack of flowering is a lack of light, which can be overcome simply by moving the plant into a more open, sunny position.

Downy mildew

The first symptoms are usually pale green marks on the upper surface of the leaves, which quite quickly turn a buff colour and correspond with a white, fluffy growth on the underside. The discoloration will eventually spread to the whole of the leaf surface and cause the leaves to drop. Infected plants should be pruned to remove the diseased areas; in severe cases the whole plant should be dug up and destroyed.

Downy mildew thrives in moist, still air, and is not usually a problem in the open garden. Those hebes that are prone to mildew, such as *H. hulkeana*,

Discoloration of leaves due to downy mildew on *Hebe* 'Autumn Glory'

Fluffy growth of mildew on lower surface of leaf

Aphid infestation on *Hebe* 'Primley Gem'

should be planted in open, exposed positions and not closely surrounded by other plants in sheltered spots. Downy mildew can, however, cause substantial losses to plants grown under cover in greenhouses or polytunnels, young plants being particularly vulnerable. To prevent this, keep the plants well spaced out and near to doors and windows to improve the air circulation around the plants.

Proprietary fungicides containing mancozeb can give some degree of control if the problem is not too far advanced, but is rarely worthwhile on plants growing outside.

Aphids

Aphids cause distortion of the young growth on hebes, the larger-leafed, faster-growing varieties being most prone to damage, particularly in mild springs when the new shoots are soft and lush. Infected shoots become distorted and frequently turn yellow, failing to develop. Flower buds that are infested will also become distorted and fail to open.

Infected plants should be treated with a proprietary insecticide or soft-soap solution, and the damaged shoots trimmed off to allow new growth to develop.

A secondary problem is often a black, sooty layer on the leaves immediately below the infestation. This is a sooty mould, which forms on the sugary juices excreted by the aphids. Once the aphids have been treated and the plants trimmed, this will usually wash off; it causes no lasting damage to the plant.

CHAPTER 10

Descriptive list of hebes

This is a listing of one hundred hebes, many of which have been mentioned in various places throughout this book. Although by no means exhaustive, this list provides a fair idea of the range of hebes available. Many of the popular ones and new varieties are readily obtainable at garden centres, while some of the more unusual species and varieties may only be found at small or specialist nurseries or at plant sales.

Descriptions include size, foliage and flower details, flowering period, hardiness and recommended uses in the garden. Particularly successful associations with other plants or colours are also suggested; these are marked ◆ at the end of each description.

PBR indicates Plant Breeders' Rights; propagation of these plants for sale without a licence is illegal.

albicans

↕ 30–45 (12–18in) ↔ 45cm (18in)

Spring	Summer	Autumn	Winter

Bushy, much-branched mound clothed in thick, grey-green leaves and covered in short, dense but well-shaped white flowers. Very hardy and free-flowering, this is a worthwhile addition to any border, attractive for both foliage and flower. It is an excellent specimen for a container.

◆ Pink, mauve and deep blue flowers, e.g. *Nepeta, Dianthus, Hyssopus*, cornflowers, lavender.

Hebe albicans

Hebe 'Amanda Cook'

albicans 'Sussex Carpet'

‡ 15–20cm (6–8in) ↔ 30–40cm (12–16 in)

Spring	Summer	Autumn	Winter

An attractive prostrate hebe with pale glaucous leaves on densely overlapping branches, bearing short white flowers. Ideal for growing bulbs underneath, or using at the front of borders, on large rock gardens or as ground cover, and good for contrast in habit and foliage colour in hebe beds.

◆ Small bulbs: crocuses, scillas, snowdrops, *Anemone blanda*

'Alicia Amherst'

‡ 1m (3ft 3in) ↔ 90cm (3ft)

Spring	Summer	Autumn	Winter

A strong-growing hybrid of *H. speciosa*, with large, glossy leaves of rich, dark green on bushy, erect growth. Young stems are green, becoming almost black as they mature and thus contributing to the overall deep colour of this rather tender hebe. Long racemes of rich violet flowers are borne over an extended period. A spectacular plant for a sheltered position in a border.

◆ *Hebe* 'Kirkii', *H.* 'Spender's Seedling', *Spiraea* 'Arguta', Japanese anemones, white asters

'Amanda Cook'

‡ 45cm (18in) ↔ 40cm (16in)

Spring	Summer	Autumn	Winter

Striking multicoloured foliage combined with dense racemes of deep violet-purple flowers make this an eye-catching shrub. It is moderately hardy and slow-growing, forming an open bush which requires regular pruning to encourage bushiness. The cream and green leaves are flushed pink and purple when young, so it is very colourful. Raised from a branch sport of 'Autumn Glory', so remove any totally green shoots that arise.

◆ Dark green or purple shrubs

amplexicaulis f. *hirta*

‡ 25–30cm (10–12in) ↔ 35cm (14in)

Spring	Summer	Autumn	Winter

A distinctive, low-growing hebe with pale green, woolly stems becoming brown and stout with age. The pale grey-green leaves are somewhat thick, edged with a reddish line and densely covered in short, white woolly hairs. Despite this, it is extremely hardy, freely producing short, dense, lateral spikes of white flowers. Unusual species for rock gardens and front of border.

◆ Purple sage, pink or white helianthemums, *Dianthus, Parahebe, Cistus*

Hebe amplexicaulis f. *hirta*

Hebe 'Amy'

× *andersonii* 'Variegata'

↕ 90–180cm (3–6ft) ↔ 90–120cm (3–4ft)

Spring	Summer	Autumn	Winter

Large, fast-growing and colourful, though hardy only in mild locations. A more or less erect shrub, height depending on conditions, it will not tolerate many degrees of frost or a prolonged severe spell, so take cuttings to overwinter. The leaves are pale grey-green or green, with irregular borders of white and pale cream. It is free-flowering, with racemes of lilac-purple flowers fading to white.

◆ Hardy fuchsias and asters for late colour

'Amy'

↕ 90cm (3ft) ↔ 45–60cm (18–24in)

Spring	Summer	Autumn	Winter

An outstanding all-year-round shrub, both for its overall glossy purple appearance and for its many racemes of deep, rich purple-violet flowers borne over a long season. A compact, upright grower, with a rounded outline, the dark purple stems are clothed in deep shiny green, purple-flushed older leaves and glossy purple young leaves. It is remarkably hardy in a fairly sheltered spot. Young pot-grown plants can be prone to mildew, but garden specimens are not usually affected.

◆ *Alchemilla mollis, Ballota pseudodictamnus, Miscanthus* for contrasting leaf textures

armstrongii

↕ 60cm (2ft) ↔ 60cm (2ft)

Spring	Summer	Autumn	Winter

A long-cultivated whipcord species now thought to be rare in the wild. The tiny yellow-green leaves closely clothe the yellowish stems, and are distinguishable from *H. ochracea* types, with which they might otherwise be confused, by being non-glossy. Branches are erect or slightly arched, and mature plants may bear terminal spikes of white flowers. A very hardy, bushy hebe for borders.

◆ Purple-leafed plants; golden flowers, e.g. *Solidago, Rudbeckia, Potentilla*

'Autumn Glory'

↕ 60cm (2ft) ↔ 60cm (2ft)

Spring	Summer	Autumn	Winter

Stunning in full flower, with short, dense racemes of rich, dark violet freely borne even when young. Hardy in all but very cold areas, it grows into a rounded, open bush. Reddish-brown stems are clothed in dark green, somewhat rounded, leaves with red margins; young leaves and shoot tips are flushed reddish-purple in winter. Lovely in borders or large pots, both the winter foliage and long flowering season make this good value all year round.

◆ *Helleborus niger*, pulsatillas, crocuses, scillas, for early flowers with the hebe's winter foliage

Hebe 'Autumn Glory'

Hebe 'Baby Marie'

'Baby Marie'

↕ 20cm (8in) ↔ 25cm (10in)

Spring	Summer	Autumn	Winter

One of the earliest to flower, and very showy when smothered in palest lilac flowers borne near the tips. Small, green leaves are closely arranged on reddish-brown stems, forming a compact, mounded bush. Moderately hardy, but best in a sheltered spot in rock gardens, raised beds, small borders or a container. Prune immediately after flowering to allow fresh growth from lower stems.

◆ Other small plants and dwarf shrubs

bishopiana

↕ 30–45cm (12–18in) ↔ 45cm (18in)

Spring	Summer	Autumn	Winter

A lovely shrub with slender purple stems carrying dark green, glossy leaves, purplish when young. Masses of pale lilac flowers, fading to white, are borne well into autumn. A valuable addition to any border or container, with good foliage colour and long-lasting, pretty flowers.

◆ *Ajuga reptans* 'Braunherz', white violas, yellow narcissi for succession of flowers

Hebe bishopiana

Hebe buchananii

'Blue Clouds'

↕ 60–90cm (2–3ft) ↔ 60–90cm (2–3ft)

Spring	Summer	Autumn	Winter

Showy, long-flowering and bushy, with deep green, shiny leaves dramatically becoming deep purple during winter. It bears two flushes of numerous long, wisteria-blue racemes. Strong-growing, it is hardy in all but the coldest areas and valuable for border or hedge due to its deep winter colour and beautiful flowers of a distinctive shade.

◆ Fresh green shrubs; soft flower colours

Hebe 'Bowles's Hybrid'

'Bowles's Hybrid'

↕ 50cm (20in) ↔ 60cm (24in)

Spring	Summer	Autumn	Winter

Easily recognizable by its very narrow, pale green leaves on light green stems with purple nodes. Free-flowering with delicate, light purple-blue, often branching, racemes that fade to white, borne in two flushes. A beautiful, distinct hebe for border or container, moderately hardy and forming an open bush. The narrow leaves give excellent contrast to broader-leafed plants.

◆ Velvety, woolly, soft leaves for contrast, e.g, *Ballota*, *Stachys*, sages

buchananii

↕ 10–15cm (4–6in) ↔ 25cm (10in)

Spring	Summer	Autumn	Winter

A low hummock of stout, tangled stems covered in small, thick, glossy, olive-green leaves. The short, dense, lateral spikes of white flowers are often partially hidden in the foliage. A totally hardy, easy hebe suitable for large troughs, raised beds and rock gardens.

◆ Colourful alpines, miniature conifers, dwarf shrubs

buchananii 'Minor'

↕ 2–4cm (¾–1½in)   ↔ 10–15cm (4–6in)

Spring	Summer	Autumn	Winter

A tiny, huddled, miniature mat or hummock of minute, leathery green leaves on very short stems, with occasional, sparse spikes of white flowers. Extremely hardy and slow-growing, so it is perfect for troughs or alpine pans to provide some evergreen structure to a miniature planting.

◆ *Thymus serpyllum* 'Elfin', tiny *Dianthus*, *Alyssum spinosum* 'Roseum'

Hebe buchananii 'Minor'

'Caledonia'

↕ 50cm (20in)   ↔ 30–40cm (12–16in)

Spring	Summer	Autumn	Winter

This stunning hebe has a long succession of violet flowers, each with a white eye, borne on branched racemes so the flower heads appear really full. It grows as a neat, erect, open bush with reddish-purple stems and small green leaves enlivened by red margins and midribs. New growth and young leaves become deep maroon during winter and spring. Excellent border or container plant for year-round interest.

◆ *Hebe* 'Bowles's Hybrid', *Cistus*, *Anthemis*, *Nepeta*, *Sedum spectabile*

'Carnea Variegata'

↕ 90–120cm (3–4ft)   ↔ 90cm (3ft)

Spring	Summer	Autumn	Winter

Colourful variegated foliage and long racemes of rich rose-pink flowers, fading to pale pink and white, make this a popular hebe for flower arrangers. A well-branched, open bush of narrow, grey-green leaves that have creamy-yellow borders, red margins, and are suffused with rosy pink in autumn. It is not very hardy, so grow in a sheltered position and take cuttings each year, or containerize and keep frost-free over winter.

◆ Deep green foliage shrubs, pink or white *Cistus*

Hebe 'Carnea Variegata'

Hebe carnosula

carnosula

‡ 20–40cm (8–16in) ↔ 20–40cm (8–16in)

Spring	Summer	Autumn	Winter

A useful, compact species for rock garden or bed, ground cover or edging, growing upright to start with but eventually becoming prostrate. The small, grey-green leaves are thick, concave and somewhat fleshy, neatly clothing pale green stems that brown with age. Short, rounded white flowers open from pinkish buds, borne near the ends of the shoots.

◆ Combine with soft colours, e.g lavender, silver thyme, blue grasses

'Christabel'

‡ 20–30cm (8–12in) ↔ 30cm (12in)

Spring	Summer	Autumn	Winter

A slow-growing, compact dome of bright emerald-green foliage, the small leaves set closely on much-branched stems. This whipcord hybrid does not flower, but makes a bright mound for rock gardens or the front of borders, or a neat specimen for a pot.

◆ Golden or deep purple flowers

chathamica

‡ 10cm (4in) ↔ 30–50cm (12–20in)

Spring	Summer	Autumn	Winter

A native of rocks near the sea in New Zealand, this is highly suited to coastal gardens, though hardy enough to grow in most areas. The slender, apple-green, trailing stems overlap to form a slightly rambling, low mound clothed thickly in fresh green leaves. Pretty white flowers tipped violet are borne in short, dense racemes. Excellent for ground cover, gravel or rock garden.

◆ *Hebe* 'County Park' and *H.* 'Wingletye' for contrasting ground cover

Hebe chathamica

colensoi

↕ 40cm (16in) ↔ 45cm (18in)

Spring	Summer	Autumn	Winter

A compact, somewhat open bush of attractive, pale glaucous green leaves set on pale green stems with mauve nodes. Free-flowering even when young, with tapering racemes of white flowers borne in dense clusters near the branch tips. Moderately hardy, it is best given some protection among other plants in small beds, front of border or rock garden.

◆ Foliage tones beautifully with soft pink and mauve, or looks cool with white, cream and primrose

'County Park'

↕ 15–20cm (6–8in) ↔ 30–40cm (12–16in)

Spring	Summer	Autumn	Winter

This attractive, prostrate hebe forms a low mound of small, grey-green, red-edged leaves on dark purple stems and bears short, crowded spikes of violet flowers. It is extremely hardy, the foliage taking on a distinctive pinkish-mauve colour in winter, and is excellent for rock gardens, borders or ground cover.

◆ Blend with pink and mauve colours, e.g. dwarf asters, veronicas, *Erigeron* 'Four Winds'

'Colwall'

↕ 5cm (2in) ↔ 10cm (4in)

Spring	Summer	Autumn	Winter

Very neat, hardy dwarf shrublet with excellent winter colour and pretty violet flowers, suitable for troughs, rock gardens and raised beds. The small, green leaves have red margins, deepening in colour in cold weather, and are set closely on reddish-brown and green stems. Plant near the side of a trough so that it can creep over to soften the edge.

◆ Small, colourful alpines

cupressoides 'Boughton Dome'

↕ 30–45cm (12–18in) ↔ 80cm (32in)

Spring	Summer	Autumn	Winter

A whipcord hebe slowly growing into a dense dome of branching grey-green stems clothed in tiny, pale grey-green leaves. Much of the foliage is juvenile, being soft to the touch and more feathery, though older plants may have a larger proportion of adult foliage, which is very small and closely pressed to the stem. This distinctive appearance means it is often mistaken for a conifer. Interesting, very hardy hebe for foliage, shape and textural interest, reaching a greater size after many years.

◆ Carpeting alpines around base, e.g. *Veronica*, *Saponaria*, *Potentilla*

Hebe colensoi

cupressoides 'Golden Dome'

↕ 23cm (9in)   ↔ 23cm (9in)

Spring	Summer	Autumn	Winter

Unusual, brightly coloured, dense hummock with
stiff, upright shoots of golden-bronze whipcord
foliage. Hardy, very slow and particularly striking
in winter, when the colour really stands out. A
good choice for raised beds, rock gardens and
small beds, and an ideal container plant.

◆ *Tulipa urumiensis* or dwarf narcissi

Hebe cupressoides 'Golden Dome'

Hebe 'Dazzler'

'Dazzler' (PBR)

↕ 30–40cm (12–16in)   ↔ 40–60cm (16–24in)

Spring	Summer	Autumn	Winter

A sport of *H.* 'Mrs Winder', this has striking,
variegated leaves of green and cream, suffused
with pinkish-purple, a coloration that is most
marked during the colder months but remains all
year. The narrow leaves are borne on slender
branches, and the semi-prostrate habit makes it an
admirable front-of-border shrub or useful as
informal ground cover. It does not flower freely.

◆ Cream, pink and lilac flowers, or deeper colours of
purple, magenta and rosy pink

Hebe cupressoides 'Boughton Dome'

Hebe decumbens

decumbens

‡ 20–30cm (8–12in) ↔ 45cm (18in)

Spring	Summer	Autumn	Winter

Distinctive, low-growing, open shrub, with slender, purple-black, shiny stems clothed in dark green, glossy, red-edged leaves. The stems spread outwards and the ends of the shoots rise upwards. The pretty white flowers, borne in dense racemes, have prominent purple anthers. An extremely hardy hebe ideal for rock gardens, borders, ground cover or alongside steps to soften the edges.

◆ *Berberis thunbergii* 'Bagatelle', *Potentilla* 'Sungold'

diosmifolia

‡ 20–30cm (8–12in) ↔ 20–30cm (8–12in)

Spring	Summer	Autumn	Winter

Beautiful, bushy plant with slender, dark green foliage on thin, arching, brownish stems, and easily identifiable by distinct, minute incisions in the leaf margins. Masses of very pale lilac flowers are borne freely in branched panicles, clustered together to form broad, rounded heads. Highly recommended as a container or patio plant, but keep frost-free over winter, as it is not at all hardy.

H. diosmifolia 'Marie' is taller, more vigorous and upright, with larger leaves and pale lilac flowers, reaching up to 60cm (2ft).

◆ Soft flower colours and silvery foliage

Hebe 'Edinensis'

'Edinensis'

‡ 30cm (12in) ↔ up to 60cm (2ft)

Spring	Summer	Autumn	Winter

A very hardy whipcord hybrid with interesting foliage, easily grown in a rock garden or small border with colourful alpines and other dwarf shrubs. The spreading, decumbent green stems are covered in tiny bright green leaves that curve stiffly outwards. It may have short spikes of white flowers occasionally, and only reaches its quoted spread after many years.

◆ *Spiraea japonica* 'Gold Mound', *Berberis thunbergii* 'Kobold'

Hebe diosmifolia 'Marie'

Hebe 'Fairfieldii'

'Edington'

↕ 1m (3ft 3in) ↔ 80cm (2ft 8in)

Spring	Summer	Autumn	Winter

Fairly hardy, bushy and free-flowering, with erect, purplish stems clothed in green leaves that are purple beneath when young and paler green when mature. Long racemes of rich violet-purple flowers, fading to paler purple, are freely produced over many weeks. This extended flowering period makes it a useful addition to a border or hebe bed, and it makes an effective hedge.

◆ Earlier-flowering deciduous shrubs, e.g. *Spiraea* 'Arguta'

'Emerald Green'

↕ 30–40cm (12–16in) ↔ 30–40cm (12–16in)

Spring	Summer	Autumn	Winter

A widespread favourite, this whipcord hybrid forms a bushy, compact dome, more or less spherical, of tiny bright green leaves, so closely spaced that the stems are largely hidden. Excellent foliage hebe for rock gardens, raised beds, front of border or container. Excessive drying wind or wet soils can discolour the foliage, so provide well-drained soil in a spot that is not too exposed.

◆ Mauve or blue trailing alpines as edging to a container-grown specimen

epacridea

↕ 10cm (4in) ↔ 20–30cm (8–12in)

Spring	Summer	Autumn	Winter

An unusual, choice species for a raised bed or large trough. The trailing, decumbent stems form a very low mound, and are mainly hidden by the thick, scale-like, stiffly recurved leaves arranged along the stems in four rows, giving them a squarish appearance. The leaves are olive-green with a faint red margin, and short spikes of white flowers are borne in dense, rounded heads. It requires sharply drained gritty soil to emulate its natural mountain habitat of scree and gravel.

◆ White- and mauve-flowering compact alpines

'Fairfieldii'

↕ 60cm (2ft) ↔ 50cm (20in)

Spring	Summer	Autumn	Winter

Sturdy, upright bush of dark purple stems and thick, dark green leaves with toothed red margins. Valuable for its comparatively early flowering, producing beautiful terminal panicles of large, showy, lilac blooms on stiff stems. A decorative hebe for a border, being reasonably hardy, thriving especially in warm and coastal areas.

◆ Valuable for its upright form among rounded or low plants

× *franciscana* 'Blue Gem'

↕ 60–90cm (2–3ft) ↔ 90cm (3ft)

Spring	Summer	Autumn	Winter

Bushy, showy hebe, free-flowering over a long period. The wide, thick leaves are dark green and glossy, paler beneath, and the dense, stout racemes of flowers are a really rich violet-blue. Easily grown, though not reliably hardy in cold areas, it is excellent for coastal regions as a border shrub or hedge

◆ *Exochorda* × *macrantha* 'The Bride', *Fuchsia* 'Margaret Brown'

× *franciscana* 'Variegata'

↕ 60cm (2ft) ↔ 60cm (2ft)

Spring	Summer	Autumn	Winter

Compact, bushy and rounded, with attractive variegated foliage. Leaves are relatively thick, coloured dark and pale green with a broad cream edging, borne on pale green stems. Large, dense, broad racemes of violet flowers fade to pinkish-lilac and white, contrasting well with the foliage. It will thrive in a warm, sheltered spot or a mild coastal garden, but is likely to be damaged elsewhere in a hard winter.

◆ White dwarf tulips, mauve pansies, in container

Hebe 'Glaucophylla Variegata'

'Glaucophylla Variegata'

↕ 60cm (2ft) ↔ 60cm (2ft)

Spring	Summer	Autumn	Winter

A bushy, upright shrub of slender, delicate appearance due to the thin, purplish stems of very small, pale leaves, which are pale grey-green with a creamy-white margin. It is reasonably hardy, bearing flowers of pale lilac-blue. Remove any all-green shoots should they arise.

◆ *Artemisia*, *Teucrium fruticans*, *Convolvulus cneorum* for a silvery, pastel colour scheme

'Great Orme'

↕ 1.4m (4ft 8in) ↔ 1.2m (4ft)

Spring	Summer	Autumn	Winter

A popular large hebe, forming a strong-growing, open bush with green leaves. It thrives in warm regions and will survive in other areas but is likely to be cut back in severe weather. Beautiful, long racemes of deep pink flowers gradually fade to white. Excellent for the back of a border, putting on a showy display over many months.

◆ Summer flowering shrubs for contrast, e.g *Potentilla*, *Viburnum*, *Escallonia*

Hebe × *franciscana* 'Variegata'

Hebe 'Greensleeves'

Hebe hectorii

'Greensleeves'

‡ 60cm (24in) ↔ 40cm (16in)

Spring	Summer	Autumn	Winter

Extremely hardy, reliable whipcord hybrid, bushy yet upright, with tiny, stiff green leaves borne less closely together than on some whipcords, so the green stems are partially visible. Unusually for a whipcord type, it flowers freely, bearing terminal white spikes. Good foliage hebe, with added advantage of flowers, for border or container.

◆ Dwarf *Berberis* and *Euonymus*, carpeting alpines, dwarf bulbs

haastii

‡ 8cm (3in) ↔ 15cm (6in) or more

Spring	Summer	Autumn	Winter

A very low-growing, decumbent species with spreading, contorted stems of thick, leathery leaves, closely overlapping and with rounded tips. Extremely variable in the wild, with three or four forms probably in cultivation. Short spikes of white flowers are borne in extremely close clusters at the tips of the shoots. A high alpine species, not easy to grow, but worth trying in gritty soil or scree, shielded from hot sun.

◆ Compact alpines requiring similar conditions

'Hagley Park'

‡ 40cm (16in) ↔ 60cm (24in)

Spring	Summer	Autumn	Winter

Hard to beat for a breathtaking display, freely producing long terminal panicles of pinkish-lilac flowers on tall, erect stems well above the foliage. Erect yet spreading bush of purplish stems bearing shiny, toothed green leaves with red margins. It is fairly hardy, grown in an open, airy position on a raised bed or rock garden to avoid its susceptibility to downy mildew.

◆ Carpeting and tufted alpines for contrast

hectorii

‡ 40cm (16in) ↔ 30cm (12in)

Spring	Summer	Autumn	Winter

A neat, attractive whipcord of distinctive appearance, with stout, rigid, cord-like branches clothed in closely adpressed leaves of yellowish-green, with paler tips, and crowded terminal spikes of white flowers. Erect when young, it becomes more decumbent with age, some branches falling outwards then turning up at the tips. Good textural interest for border or rock garden.

◆ Foliage with contrasting textures, e.g. *Alchemilla, Sedum*

Hebe 'Heidi'

'Heidi'

$\updownarrow$ 30cm (12in) $\leftrightarrow$ 30cm (12in)

Spring	Summer	Autumn	Winter

Neat, dwarf bush with small, dark green leaves, forming a bushy, erect shape though slightly open. Young leaves and tips are coloured deep purple in winter, and it is late-flowering, bearing numerous neat, mauve flowers, even during winter in mild spells. An attractive addition to a small border for its coloured foliage and late flowers.

◆ *Hebe recurva* and *H.* 'County Park' to form a contrasting group

Hebe 'James Platt'

'Hielan Lassie'

$\updownarrow$ 1m (3ft 3in) $\leftrightarrow$ 80cm (2ft 8in)

Spring	Summer	Autumn	Winter

Fairly compact bush of green leaves on purplish stems; purplish undersides and margins of young leaves provide additional colour. A reasonably hardy hebe for borders, with attractive flowers of deep violet-purple fading to white.

◆ White and yellow flowers for contrast

hulkeana

$\updownarrow$ 45cm (18in) $\leftrightarrow$ 40cm (16in)

Spring	Summer	Autumn	Winter

One of the most showy, this is an open, sprawling shrub of dark green, toothed, glossy leaves carried on dark purple stems. Long, lax panicles of white or lilac flowers put on a stunning display and give the plant a dainty, airy appearance. It thrives in open, sunny positions that are windswept or fully exposed, as in its natural habitat, so don't surround it with other plants in a sheltered spot, where it is likely to suffer from downy mildew.

◆ *Armeria maritima, Parahebe*

'James Platt'

$\updownarrow$ 60cm (24in) $\leftrightarrow$ 40cm (16in)

Spring	Summer	Autumn	Winter

Unusual and hardy, with a markedly upright growing habit. The dark purple-brown stems are tinged red and clothed in widely spaced, slightly concave, small leaves of dull green with red margins. Free-flowering, bearing many short racemes of blue flowers at the ends of the branches.

◆ *Escallonia* 'Gwendolyn Anley' behind, *Centaurea bella* and *Geranium sànguineum* var. *striatum* in front

Hebe 'Jasper'

'Jasper'

↕ 15–20cm (6–8in) ↔ 20cm (8in)

Spring	Summer	Autumn	Winter

A low, bright green cushion of tiny, glossy, fairly thick leaves on very densely branched green stems. The bright foliage and pretty white flowers enhance alpine plantings in rock gardens and raised beds. It is hardy, and small enough to plant in a trough or use for very dwarf hedging.

 Thymus serpyllum 'Minimus', *Geranium dalmaticum*, *Sisyrinchium idahoense* in a trough

'Joan Lewis'

↕ 70–80cm (28–32in) ↔ 70cm (28in)

Spring	Summer	Autumn	Winter

Sturdy, strongly growing bush of fairly open habit, bearing sessile (i.e. not stalked) grey-green leaves with slightly reddish margins. They are quite thick and stiff, spreading outwards from the stems. Short, rounded spikes of densely clustered flowers are white with a faint pink tinge. A reasonably hardy, free-flowering hebe for borders.

Pink flowers that pick up the tinge in its blooms, e.g. *Cistus* 'Silver Pink', *Spiraea japonica* 'Shirobana', *Diascia*

'Kirkii'

↕ 1.8m (6ft) ↔ 1.8m (6ft) or more

Spring	Summer	Autumn	Winter

A large, strong-growing, hardy hebe ideal for the back of a border, with erect, well-branched stems that turn purplish-brown as they mature. The glossy green leaves are a suitable foil for the long, slender white flower racemes.

Clematis viticella forms to scramble through and flower in late summer

'Lindsayi'

↕ 90cm (3ft) ↔ 60cm (2ft)

Spring	Summer	Autumn	Winter

Distinct, compact habit, with mid-green to greyish-green leaves on dark purple, upright stems. An excellent flowering hebe, covered in dense, rounded heads of closely packed, pale pinkish-lilac blooms that gradually fade to white. Neat enough for a container, it also makes an effective border shrub.

Soft blue *Caryopteris*, silvery *Convolvulus cneorum* and lavenders, white *Potentilla fruticosa* 'Manchu'

'Loganioides'

↕ 20–25cm (8–10in) ↔ 20cm (8in)

Spring	Summer	Autumn	Winter

An interesting small whipcord hybrid with tiny green leaves, often brownish-green, becoming attractively bronze-tinted in winter. White, pink-veined flowers, comparatively large for the size of the plant, are borne near the tips. It tends to open out with age, with the branchlets turning upwards and older stems often rooting into the soil. Ideal for rock gardens, gravel beds or large troughs.

Penstemon pinifolius, *Campanula garganica* 'Dickson's Gold' (red and mauve flowers, golden foliage)

Hebe macrantha

'Lopen'

$\updownarrow$ 1.5m (5ft) $\leftrightarrow$ 1.5m (5ft)

Spring	Summer	Autumn	Winter

Attractive, moderately hardy, variegated sport of 'Midsummer Beauty', ideal for the back of a border. The leaves are bright green with a broad, creamy-yellow margin, and young leaves have purple midribs. It has an extended flowering period, bearing very long racemes of light violet-purple flowers that fade to white.

◆ Glossy green *Choisya ternata*, white *Buddleja davidii* 'Peace'

lycopodioides

$\updownarrow$ 8–20cm (3–8in) $\leftrightarrow$ 15–20cm (6–8in)

Spring	Summer	Autumn	Winter

Variable yellowish-green whipcord with a stiff, bushy habit. Tiny overlapping leaves are adpressed closely to the distinctly squared branchlets. Much of the foliage is often juvenile, turning bronze in winter. Low, bushy plant, becoming decumbent, with terminal spikes of white flowers, it is an extremely hardy species for troughs and raised beds.

◆ *Gentiana acaulis, Potentilla eriocarpa, Hebe* 'Youngii'

macrantha

$\updownarrow$ 30–60cm (1–2ft) $\leftrightarrow$ 40cm (16in)

Spring	Summer	Autumn	Winter

Distinct species with very showy flowers, though borne only over about three weeks. The sparse, upright stems form a straggling, woody bush with toothed, leathery green leaves. This untidy growth habit is offset by the unique flowers – large, glistening white, in short racemes of up to eight flowers near the branch tips. Thrives in a sheltered position, being fairly hardy but liable to damage in severe weather. The base tends to become woody and bare, so disguise with low plants around it.

◆ Carpeting plants around base, e.g. *Geranium, Campanula, Nepeta*'

'Margret' (PBR)

$\updownarrow$ 30–45cm (12–18in) $\leftrightarrow$ 45cm (18in)

Spring	Summer	Autumn	Winter

Compact, low, rounded bush of shiny, bright green foliage, with a profusion of sky-blue flowers that fade progressively to light blue and then white. A free-flowering, hardy dwarf hebe for the front of a border or container, harmonizing with other soft-coloured plants.

◆ *Dianthus, Nepeta*, silver foliage plants

Hebe 'Margret'

'Marjorie'

↕ 1m (3ft 3in)   ↔ 1m (3ft 3in)

Spring	Summer	Autumn	Winter

This hardy hebe has long been a favourite in British gardens, making a wide, bushy shrub of green leaves that are glossy on both surfaces. It is free-flowering, with light mauve-blue flowers. A border plant to display among deeper-coloured shrubs.

◆ *Osmanthus heterophyllus, Philadelphus* 'Manteau d'Hermine', *Euonymus fortunei* 'Emerald Gaiety'

'Midsummer Beauty'

↕ 1.5m (5ft)   ↔ 1.2m (4ft)

Spring	Summer	Autumn	Winter

Another very popular hebe, this is a large, strong-growing bush with erect, purple-tinged, pale green stems and bright green foliage. Young leaves are purplish underneath. A reasonably hardy form for the back of the border, providing plenty of colour with its mass of flowers. These are very long, the flowers crowded together on the raceme, and are light violet-purple, fading to white.

◆ *Hebe* 'Great Orme', *H. salicifolia, H.* 'Sapphire'

Hebe 'Mist Maiden'

'Mist Maiden'

↕ 40cm (16in)   ↔ 50–60cm (20–24in)

Spring	Summer	Autumn	Winter

A low mound of wide-spreading brownish-purple stems clothed in green leaves. It has two flowering periods, freely producing long, delicate racemes of very pale lilac flowers that fade to white, displaying a misty effect reflected in its name. Not widely grown, but a desirable hardy hebe for the front of a border.

◆ Deep purple and mauve flowers, e.g. *Lavandula angustifolia* 'Imperial Gem', dwarf asters

'Monica'

↕ 50cm (20in)   ↔ 45cm (18in)

Spring	Summer	Autumn	Winter

A hardy hebe, easily pleased, with upright purple stems of small, green, red-margined leaves. Excellent for the middle of a border, with pinkish-purple spikes of flowers.

◆ *Hebe albicans, H.* 'Autumn Glory' for contrast

'Mrs Winder'

↕ 1m (3ft 3in)   ↔ 90cm (3ft)

Spring	Summer	Autumn	Winter

A widely grown, very hardy hebe of bushy, rounded shape and densely branched. The shiny, dark green leaves are flushed purple, becoming more deeply coloured in winter, transforming it into a dark reddish-purple foliage shrub. Flowers are not freely produced; dense racemes of violet-blue, when they do appear, are borne late and fade to white. An excellent hedging plant or background shrub.

◆ Plant behind *Ceanothus thyrsiflorus* var. *repens, Cistus, Lavandula*

Hebe ochracea 'James Stirling'

ochracea 'James Stirling'

⇕ 40cm (16in)   ↔ 60cm (24in)

Spring	Summer	Autumn	Winter

Handsome, extremely hardy, slow-growing whipcord with dense, overlapping branches that arch strongly outwards to form a distinctive flat-topped shape. Tiny, scale-like leaves of a wonderful old-gold colour are firmly pressed against stout stems. Sparse white flowers may be sporadically borne on mature plants. Older plants tend to lose their leaves in the centre, revealing stout, woody branches. Excellent colour and textural interest for border, large rock garden or container.

◆ Gold and purple flowers and foliage

'Neil's Choice'

⇕ 1.3m (4ft 4in)   ↔ 1.3m (4ft 4in)

Spring	Summer	Autumn	Winter

A hardy, bushy shrub for border or hedge, the dark reddish-purple stems carrying thin, dark green leaves with reddish-purple margins and midribs. Young leaves are also this deeper colour. The long flowering season lasts well into winter in favourable weather, with long racemes of rich violet-purple flowers. Excellent for all-year interest, but especially for late colour.

◆ Early-flowering shrubs, e.g. *Spiraea* 'Arguta', Deutzia

Hebe 'Nicola's Blush'

'Nicola's Blush'

⇕ 60cm (2ft)   ↔ 60cm (2ft)

Spring	Summer	Autumn	Winter

Hugely popular, though only introduced about 20 years ago, this hardy, bushy hebe is renowned for its exceptionally long, free-flowering season, often continuing into winter in mild spells. The mid-green leaves have red margins and are often tinged purple and bronze in winter. The lovely pink flowers, borne in broad racemes, gradually fade to white, giving a two-tone effect. Plant in the border or in a large container.

◆ *Hebe* 'Blue Clouds', *H.* 'Bowles's Hybrid', *H.* 'Marjorie'

Hebe odora 'New Zealand Gold'

Hebe 'Petra's Pink'

odora 'New Zealand Gold'

↕ 60–100cm (2ft–2ft 3in)　↔ 60cm (2ft)

Spring	Summer	Autumn	Winter

Neat, erect and bushy, with yellowish stems clothed in bright green, shiny, stiff leaves. In some soil conditions, the younger leaves become distinctly yellow, showing up particularly brightly in winter. Extremely hardy, with white spikes of flowers, it is a good evergreen background plant and makes a neat, closely knit hedge.

◆ Golden flowers (*Coreopsis, Solidago*) or mauve flowers (scabious, asters, campanulas)

'Petra's Pink'

↕ 30cm (12in)　↔ 50cm (20in)

Spring	Summer	Autumn	Winter

A lovely dwarf hebe forming a spreading, rather open, low mound of purple stems carrying dark green leaves with purplish-red margins, enhanced by deeper purplish tones in winter. The neat pink flowers contrast beautifully with the dark foliage. It needs regular pruning, particularly when young and after flowering, to maintain a compact, bushy habit and prevent it becoming woody and sprawling. Plant at the front of a border, in a rock garden or as ground cover.

◆ *Hebe recurva, H.* 'Wiri Cloud', *H.* 'Margret' for a contrasting group

pauciramosa

↕ 30–50cm (12–20in)　↔ 30cm (12in)

Spring	Summer	Autumn	Winter

An interesting, hardy hebe, not often seen, with sparsely branched, upright stems clad in small, stiff, shiny green leaves. A neat species for borders or containers, it has a rounded outline due to the few branches arising mainly from near the base. It flowers well, bearing spikes of white blooms in clusters near the branch tips, often well into autumn. Usually found in moist or even wet soil in the wild.

◆ Helianthemums, parahebes, bushy thymes

Hebe pauciramosa

Hebe pinguifolia 'Pagei'

'Pewter Dome'

‡ 30–45cm (12–18in) ↔ 30–45cm (12–18in)

Spring	Summer	Autumn	Winter

Excellent grey foliage plant for border, rock garden or container, making a stocky, rounded dome. Fully hardy, the grey-green leaves are borne on much-branched stems, but it really comes into its own when flowering begins. The white flowers are borne in very dense, short racemes of a neat, tapering shape, smothering the whole plant.

◆ White and pink dwarf bulbs

'Pimeba'

‡ 30cm (12in) ↔ 30cm (12in)

Spring	Summer	Autumn	Winter

Very attractive dwarf hebe with dark stems of red-margined, grey-green leaves. The tips of the shoots and young leaves also turn red in winter. Free-flowering, with dense spikes of purple-blue flowers fading to pale lilac. Easy and reliable, with an open, upright habit, for small beds, rock gardens and containers.

◆ *Hebe decumbens*, *Berberis thunbergii* 'Kobold', *Spiraea japonica* 'Bullata'

pimeleoides 'Quicksilver'

‡ 40–60cm (16–24in) ↔ 50–70cm (20–28in)

Spring	Summer	Autumn	Winter

A popular hebe, often planted in groups as shrubby ground cover, but also making a fine specimen shrub. Very hardy, with an open habit, it has semi-prostrate, sprawling though stiff stems that are slender and almost black. The distinctly silvery leaves are bright, tiny and widely spaced, adding to the open, airy appearance. The small flowers are pale blue. Useful foliage for flower arrangers.

◆ Magenta geraniums and lychnis, deep pink veronicas and asters

pimeleoides var. *minor*

‡ 5cm (2in) ↔ 10–15cm (4–6in)

Spring	Summer	Autumn	Winter

Minute, almost prostrate, creeping shrublet with slender, dark stems, tiny grey-green, almost silvery, leaves and pale violet flowers. A reasonably hardy little plant for troughs and pans, combined with slow, compact alpines.

◆ Tiny *Dianthus*, *Silene acaulis*, *Thymus serpyllum* 'Minimus'

pinguifolia 'Pagei'

↕ 15–20cm (6–8in)　↔ 20–30cm (8–12in)

Spring	Summer	Autumn	Winter

A well-known, hardy dwarf hebe, forming low, carpeting mounds smothered in dense white spikes of flowers. The grey-green leaves are slightly concave and rounded, carried on pale green stems that mature to purple and brown. Effective ground cover, the stems often rooting where they touch the soil. *H. pinguifolia* 'Sutherlandii' has a denser, more upright habit, up to 40cm (20in), later becoming decumbent, and has pale grey-green leaves and white flowers. Plant either of these in borders, rock gardens and containers, or as an edging alongside paths.

◆ Soft pink, mauve and white flowers for a subtle colour scheme

'Pink Elephant'

↕ 60cm (24in)　↔ 45cm (18in)

Spring	Summer	Autumn	Winter

A colourful sport from *H.* 'Red Edge', slowly forming a compact, bushy shrub for borders or containers. The leaves are a unique blend of buttery-yellow and green variegation, tipped pink, becoming suffused with burgundy in winter, giving a stunning coloration. It bears white flowers, but the main attraction is the foliage.

◆ Dwarf white spring bulbs

'Pink Paradise' (PBR)

↕ 40cm (16in)　↔ 30–40cm (12–16in)

Spring	Summer	Autumn	Winter

Low-growing, bushy hebe carrying mid-green leaves with red margins on dark stems. It bears lovely pink flowers that open from deeper pink buds, and is free-flowering over many months. An attractive addition for the border.

◆ Reddish-purple foliage, pink and lilac flowers

Hebe 'Pink Elephant'

'Primley Gem'

‡ 60cm (24in)   ↔ 45cm (18in)

Spring	Summer	Autumn	Winter

Crowded reddish-brown stems bear distinctive, slightly wavy-edged leaves that are matt green with a red margin. Young leaves are reddish beneath, and leaves take on pinkish-purple tints in winter. Pretty mauve-blue flowers fading to pale lilac are borne in quite dense racemes near the shoot tips. A long-flowering, reasonably hardy hebe with an attractive shape, well clothed in foliage, suitable for borders or large containers. It can also still be found under the name 'Margery Fish'.

◆ Bushy hebes with foliage contrast, e.g. 'Wiri Mist', 'Autumn Glory', 'Bowles's Hybrid'

Winter foliage of *Hebe* 'Primley Gem'

Hebe 'Primley Gem'

propinqua

‡ 15cm (6in)   ↔ 30cm (12in)

Spring	Summer	Autumn	Winter

Dwarf whipcord with much-branched, threadlike, yellowish-green stems forming a dense, flat-topped cushion. It forms wide mats in the wild, but in cultivation remains more compact. The tiny, bright yellow-green leaves clothe the stems so closely they are more or less hidden, and little white spikes of flowers are carried near the tips. Ideal for rock garden or peat bed, preferring moist soil protected from scorching midday sun.

◆ Small ferns, dwarf rhododendrons

rakaiensis

‡ 70cm (2ft 4in)   ↔ 90cm (3ft) or more

Spring	Summer	Autumn	Winter

Widely grown, this hardy species forms a dome of bright green, slightly glossy, leaves and carries white flowers. It can grow much wider than its height, and is fairly dense, so is useful for large areas of ground cover or for hedging, as well as adding evergreen structure to a border.

◆ Colourful flowering shrubs, e.g. *Potentilla*, *Weigela*

Hebe raoulii var. *pentasepala*

Hebe 'Red Edge'

raoulii var. *pentasepala*

↕ 20cm (8in) ↔ 15cm (6in)

Spring	Summer	Autumn	Winter

A choice, pretty hebe with upright, dark, slender stems of small, red-edged, dark green leaves. Branching terminal spikes of pink buds open into white or pale lilac flowers. *H. raoulii* var. *maccaskillii* is also tiny and slow-growing, with a more compact, bushy habit and spikes of lilac flowers. Both are reasonably hardy, though rarely seen, and small enough for troughs and raised beds.

◆ Compact alpines, e.g. tiny *Dianthus*, *Sisyrinchium idahoense*, *Thymus serpyllum* 'Elfin'

'Red Edge'

↕ 40–60cm (16–24in) ↔ 40cm (16in)

Spring	Summer	Autumn	Winter

This well-known hebe is distinguished by dark red margins around the grey-green leaves, which in cold weather become suffused with maroon. Shoot tips and young leaves are particularly deeply coloured, transforming the plant into a really striking feature. It is a very hardy, dense, compact bush, the green stems ageing to brown, and carries pale lilac flowers, though these can be sparse. An attractive form for winter interest in borders or containers.

◆ *Perovskia* 'Blue Spire', *Aster amellus* 'Veilchenkönigin', *Geranium macrorrhizum* 'Album', for stunning late colour

recurva

↕ 30–40cm (12–16in) ↔ 30cm (12in)

Spring	Summer	Autumn	Winter

Lovely, elegant, free-flowering dwarf hebe with reddish-brown stems carrying closely-spaced, narrow, grey, sickle-shaped leaves. Many white flowers are borne in crowded, slender racemes, covering the bush. Reasonably hardy, with a neat, tidy growth habit, this is a valuable small, late-flowering plant for the rock garden or border.

◆ *Cistus × danseraui* 'Decumbens', *Centaurea bella*, dwarf lavenders

Hebe recurva

rigidula

↕ 30–40cm (12–16in) ↔ 25cm (10in)

Spring	Summer	Autumn	Winter

Very neat and free-flowering, the much-branched, yellow-green stems forming an upright shrub with green, glossy leaves that are greyish underneath. Masses of white flowers are freely borne on short, closely arranged racemes. It is reasonably hardy, remaining very compact if pruned each year immediately after flowering. Lovely small shrub for border, small bed or pot, and makes a wonderful dwarf flowering hedge.

◆ Small pinks, parahebes, veronicas

Hebe rigidula

'Rosie' (PBR)

↕ 60cm (2ft) ↔ 80cm (2ft 8in)

Spring	Summer	Autumn	Winter

Bushy, compact, hardy form renowned for its bright pink flowers, fading to pale pink and then white. These are borne in dense racemes, often with flushes appearing until early winter. The dark green leaves are purplish when young, and the bush can grow quite wide. A good, pink-flowered hebe for border or large container.

◆ *Fuchsia magellanica* 'Versicolor', *Sedum* 'Ruby Glow', *Artemisia* 'Powis Castle'

salicifolia

↕ 1.8m (6ft) ↔ 1.2m (4ft)

Spring	Summer	Autumn	Winter

Commonly grown, large, bushy hebe with upright, pale yellow-green stems and long, willowy, light green leaves. Fairly hardy, it is ideal for the back of a border or a tall hedge in mild areas, and rarely sustains long-term damage in colder regions. It has a long flowering season, bearing many long, drooping racemes of pale lilac-blue flowers fading to white. It is a parent of many garden hybrids.

◆ *Escallonia* 'Donard Seedling', *Viburnum* × *burkwoodii* 'Anne Russell', *Syringa vulgaris* 'Congo'

Colourful young shoots of *Hebe* 'Sapphire'

'Sapphire'

↕ 1m (3ft 3in) ↔ 75cm (2ft 6in)

Spring	Summer	Autumn	Winter

Very colourful in winter and spring, this free-flowering hebe is upright, bushy and well branched, with attractive red-flushed foliage and bronzed, reddish midribs. The colour deepens considerably and appears almost purple overall during winter. Long, dense racemes of rosy purple flowers are borne over a long period. Reasonably hardy, this variety adds both foliage and flower colour to a border.

◆ *Cistus laurifolius, Philadelphus* 'Belle Etoile', *Fuchsia* 'Mrs Popple'

Hebe 'Sapphire'

'Silver Dollar'

↕ 60cm (2ft) ↔ 60cm (2ft)

Spring	Summer	Autumn	Winter

A fairly recent introduction, forming a low, spreading mound of green and silver variegated leaves. Each leaf has a narrow red margin, and in winter the shoot tips become burgundy in colour. A lovely, fairly hardy, variegated hebe for a border or large container, the foliage even more attractive with its winter coloration.

◆ Dark or reddish foliage, e.g. *Hebe* 'Caledonia', *Berberis thunbergii* 'Bagatelle'

'Simon Delaux'

↕ 1m (3ft 3in) ↔ 80cm (2ft 8in)

Spring	Summer	Autumn	Winter

Well-known, large *H. speciosa* hybrid, desirable because of its beautiful long racemes of crimson flowers, making a showy, long-flowering border plant in suitable conditions. Bushy and upright, it is unfortunately not very hardy at all, tolerating only light frosts, so is suitable only for mild areas. In colder areas, take cuttings to overwinter in frost-free conditions.

◆ *Buddleja* 'Lochinch', *Hebe* 'Spender's Seedling'

Hebe speciosa 'La Seduisante'

speciosa 'La Seduisante'

↕ 1m (3ft 3in) ↔ 80cm (2ft 8in)

Spring	Summer	Autumn	Winter

Beautiful, showy hebe of bushy, upright growth with stunning flowers, for planting in borders. The leaves are green and glossy, purplish beneath when young, and the long racemes of flowers are a distinctive reddish-purple, borne over a long period in favourable conditions. It is not at all reliably hardy, tolerating only light frost, so take cuttings to overwinter.

◆ White- and pink-flowered shrubs, e.g. *Olearia*, *Potentilla*, *Deutzia*, *Philadelphus*

'Spender's Seedling'

↕ 1m (3ft 3in) ↔ 90cm (3ft)

Spring	Summer	Autumn	Winter

Hardy, reliable and showy, this is a bushy, erect, free-flowering hebe for the border. The dark green leaves, with matt surfaces, form a good background for the slender racemes of white flowers borne in profusion over many months. Easy to grow, it associates with a wide range of other shrubs.

◆ *Spiraea* 'Arguta', *Deutzia* × *rosea*, *Cistus* 'Silver Pink' and roses, for a succession of flowers

subalpina

↕ 40–60cm (16–24in) ↔ 40–50cm (16–20in)

Spring	Summer	Autumn	Winter

Reliable, hardy species with relatively long, narrow leaves of bright glossy green on upright stems with markedly purple nodes. It is well branched, forming a bushy shrub and bearing crowded racemes of white flowers. The glossy foliage and free-flowering habit make this an attractive small shrub for a border or pot, or for a compact hedge.

◆ Fits in with other small shrubs, perennials and grasses in any colour scheme

subsimilis var. *astonii*

↕ 15cm (6in) ↔ 25cm (10in)

Spring	Summer	Autumn	Winter

Unusual, compact, miniature whipcord that grows into a low, lax hummock. The bright yellowish-green leaves are closely adpressed, except at the tips, to the thin, branching stems. Short, terminal spikes of a few white flowers may be produced. A choice species for a trough or pan, but it can be difficult to please, resenting full sun or drying out, which can rapidly brown the foliage.

◆ Neat, compact alpines

'Tiny Tot'

‡ 10cm (4in) ↔ 10cm (4in)

Spring	Summer	Autumn	Winter

Diminutive, compact form raised from a seedling of *H.* 'Youngii', with branching, huddled, very short green stems. The tiny green leaves are densely overlapping, but spread away from the stems, and it bears little violet-blue flowers. Being so tiny, it is ideal for a trough or pan, and is moderately hardy.

◆ *Dianthus* 'Berlin Snow', *Veronica prostrata* 'Nana', *Sempervivum arachnoideum* var. *bryoides*

topiaria

‡ 30–60m (1–2ft) ↔ 60–90cm (2–3ft)

Spring	Summer	Autumn	Winter

This grows into a perfectly rounded, compact, wide hummock. It is completely hardy, with small, closely packed, grey-green leaves, making a very effective specimen shrub or foliage plant for the border. White flowers are distributed unevenly and sparsely over the bush, almost hidden in the foliage. Excellent as low ground cover, planted in groups, and as a hedge, responding well to regular trimming.

◆ Soft pink and mauve flowers, e.g. *Centaurea bella*, *Diascia*, lavenders

Hebe vernicosa

vernicosa

‡ 30–40cm (12–16in) ↔ 40cm (16in)

Spring	Summer	Autumn	Winter

Beautiful, neat and free-flowering, this forms a compact, rounded bush. The small, dark green, glossy leaves are attractive all year, and slender racemes of pale lilac flowers, fading to white, are borne in profusion. A very hardy hebe, ideal for many uses and highly recommended for borders, large rock gardens or pots. It makes a compact dwarf hedge with its neat foliage and pretty flowers.

◆ *Linaria purpurea* 'Canon Went', *Potentilla fruticosa* 'Manchu', silvery-blue *Festuca*

Hebe topiaria

'Watson's Pink'

↕ 90cm (3ft) ↔ 90cm (3ft)

Spring	Summer	Autumn	Winter

An attractive pink-flowered hebe for the border,
forming a bushy shrub of green foliage. Young
leaves have a purplish tinge. The flowers are borne
in two flushes, and it is noticeable that the buds at
the tip of the raceme do not develop and open.
Although reasonably hardy, it can be damaged in
severe weather.

◆ Soft colours, e.g. *Geranium macrorrhizum* 'Album',
Perovskia 'Blue Spire', white delphiniums

'White Gem'

↕ 40–60cm (16–24in) ↔ 40–60cm (16–24in)

Spring	Summer	Autumn	Winter

Dense, bushy dome, with neat, fresh, light green
leaves that are quite thick and slightly glossy.
White flowers with dark anthers are borne near
the tips, but are often just scattered unevenly over
the bush. Left as a specimen shrub, it forms a low,
wide mound; or makes effective ground cover
planted as a group. It responds well to clipping,
so makes an excellent low hedge.

◆ Colourful flowers, e.g. *Ceanothus, Caryopteris, Potentilla*

Hebe 'White Heather'

'White Heather'

↕ 60–90cm (2–3ft) ↔ 60–90cm (2–3ft)

Spring	Summer	Autumn	Winter

A lovely flowering hebe, with good-sized, quite
broad racemes of white flowers, the pale lilac
anthers adding a touch of soft colour. The flowers
are displayed effectively against the shiny green
foliage, and are borne in profusion. It forms a
bushy, rounded, well-shaped shrub, equally
effective in the border or in a container.

◆ Stronger-coloured hebes, e.g. 'Autumn Glory', 'Monica',
'Wiri Charm'

Hebe 'White Gem'

'Wingletye'

‡ 20cm (8in) ↔ 30–45cm (12–18in) or more

Spring	Summer	Autumn	Winter

Excellent ground-cover hebe, with decumbent, spreading stems, turning markedly upwards at the tips and clothed in small, glaucous leaves. Lilac flowers are freely borne, held well above the foliage, their colour harmonizing beautifully with that of the leaves. Totally hardy, it forms effective ground cover either individually or in groups, and looks wonderful in soft colour schemes.

◆ *Geranium sanguineum* var. *striatum, Salvia officinalis* 'Tricolor'

Hebe 'Wingletye'

'Wiri Charm'

‡ 45cm (18in) ↔ 40cm (16in)

Spring	Summer	Autumn	Winter

Bushy, upright and somewhat spreading to give a rounded outline, this is clothed in dark green leaves with red midribs. These contrast nicely with the reddish-brown stems. It has lovely flowers of rosy purple, carried in abundance. A very distinctive hebe in shape, foliage and flower colour, contrasting with the softer hebe colours in borders or containers.

◆ *Aster novi-belgii* (dwarf) in rosy or purple shades

Hebe 'Wiri Charm'

Hebe 'Wiri Cloud'

Hebe 'Wiri Mist'

'Wiri Cloud'

↕ 30–40cm (12–16in) ↔ 30–40cm (12–16in)

Spring	Summer	Autumn	Winter

A bushy, rounded plant with well-branched, yellow-green stems thickly clothed in small, golden-green leaves. Many neat, sugar-pink flowers are carried tidily over the bush. An extremely attractive small shrub for pots or the border, with a particularly distinctive combination of foliage and flower colour.

◆ White, pink and soft mauve flowers for harmony, or purple and rosy pink for contrast

'Wiri Mist'

↕ 60cm (2ft) ↔ 60cm (2ft)

Spring	Summer	Autumn	Winter

Attractive, rounded bush with outward-spreading stems giving a distinctive layered effect. The stems are well clothed in fresh green foliage, and many dense, sturdy, white flowers of a good shape are carried. This is a really well-shaped, free-flowering hebe for use in borders or pots.

◆ *Hebe* 'Primley Gem', *H.* 'Autumn Glory', *Weigela florida* 'Foliis Purpureis'

Hebe 'Wiri Dawn'

'Wiri Dawn'

↕ 40cm (16in) ↔ 40cm (16in)

Spring	Summer	Autumn	Winter

Another distinctive hebe in this series, forming a low mound of very slender, shiny, light green leaves. Young stems are yellow-green, ageing to dark brown. Elegant, slender racemes of rose-pink flowers are borne over a long period. A beautiful hebe with a delicate appearance, ideal for the front of a border or small bed.

◆ *Nepeta*, *Geranium sanguineum* 'Album', *Veronica spicata*

Hebe 'Youngii'

'Youngii'

‡ 15–20cm (6–8in) ↔ 30–60cm (1–2ft)

Spring	Summer	Autumn	Winter

Low, decumbent, spreading shrublet with dark,
almost black, wiry stems and shiny green,
somewhat stiff leaves with red margins, well
spaced on the stems. It carries numerous, very
pretty flowers of violet, fading to white, in short,
loose racemes near the tips. Very low but wide-
spreading, it is a popular hebe (for many years
known as *H.* 'Carl Teschner') for rock gardens,
small beds, ground cover or edging.

◆ *Campanula carpatica, Penstemon pinifolius, Scutellaria
alpina*

About the authors

Chris Wheeler has an honours degree in Agriculture, and was involved in training and landscaping, including much tree planting in the aftermath of the Great Storm of 1987, before he and Valerie started their own nursery.

He has considerable experience in growing plants and teaching gardeners at all levels how to get the most out of their gardens. He lectures widely and runs a variety of practical gardening courses, and is chairman of a local training group.

A self-taught photographer, Chris specializes in environmental subjects, contributing to picture libraries and specialist publications.

Valerie Wheeler gained an honours degree in Horticultural Science at Wye College, London University, then worked in research and commercial horticulture.

She has many years' experience in designing and supplying the plants for sinks, containers and raised beds, her postal design service being available nationwide. She writes and produces all the nursery's catalogues and cultural notes, and has written a number of articles for gardening publications. She has also written booklets on sink plants and dwarf hebes for the nursery's customers.

Aside from gardening, Valerie enjoys all forms of embroidery, much of which adorns the walls at home.

Their mail-order nursery, Siskin Plants, specializes in dwarf hardy plants, particularly trough plants, sempervivums and dwarf hebes. Chris and Valerie hold the National Collection of Dwarf Hebes (East Anglia), containing over one hundred species and cultivars.

They are the authors of *Sink & Container Gardening using Dwarf Hardy Plants* and *Alpine Gardening*, both published by GMC Publications.

Hebe topiaria

Index

Pages highlighted in **bold** include illustrations
of plants.

TITLES AVAILABLE FROM
GMC Publications

BOOKS

WOODCARVING

Beginning Woodcarving	GMC Publications
Carving Architectural Detail in Wood: The Classical Tradition	
	Frederick Wilbur
Carving Birds & Beasts	GMC Publications
Carving the Human Figure: Studies in Wood and Stone	Dick Onians
Carving Nature: Wildlife Studies in Wood	Frank Fox-Wilson
Carving on Turning	Chris Pye
Decorative Woodcarving	Jeremy Williams
Elements of Woodcarving	Chris Pye
Essential Woodcarving Techniques	Dick Onians
Lettercarving in Wood: A Practical Course	Chris Pye
Making & Using Working Drawings for Realistic Model Animals	
	Basil F. Fordham
Power Tools for Woodcarving	David Tippey
Relief Carving in Wood: A Practical Introduction	Chris Pye
Understanding Woodcarving in the Round	GMC Publications
Useful Techniques for Woodcarvers	GMC Publications
Woodcarving: A Foundation Course	Zoë Gertner
Woodcarving for Beginners	GMC Publications
Woodcarving Tools, Materials & Equipment (New Edition in 2 vols.)	Chris Pye

WOODTURNING

Adventures in Woodturning	David Springett
Bowl Turning Techniques Masterclass	Tony Boase
Chris Child's Projects for Woodturners	Chris Child
Colouring Techniques for Woodturners	Jan Sanders
Contemporary Turned Wood: New Perspectives in a Rich Tradition	
	Ray Leier, Jan Peters & Kevin Wallace
The Craftsman Woodturner	Peter Child
Decorating Turned Wood: The Maker's Eye	Liz & Michael O'Donnell
Decorative Techniques for Woodturners	Hilary Bowen
Illustrated Woodturning Techniques	John Hunnex
Intermediate Woodturning Projects	GMC Publications
Keith Rowley's Woodturning Projects	Keith Rowley
Making Screw Threads in Wood	Fred Holder
Turned Boxes: 50 Designs	Chris Stott
Turning Green Wood	Michael O'Donnell
Turning Pens and Pencils	Kip Christensen & Rex Burningham
Useful Woodturning Projects	GMC Publications
Woodturning: Bowls, Platters, Hollow Forms, Vases, Vessels, Bottles, Flasks, Tankards, Plates	GMC Publications
Woodturning: A Foundation Course (New Edition)	Keith Rowley
Woodturning: A Fresh Approach	Robert Chapman
Woodturning: An Individual Approach	Dave Regester
Woodturning: A Source Book of Shapes	John Hunnex
Woodturning Jewellery	Hilary Bowen
Woodturning Masterclass	Tony Boase
Woodturning Techniques	GMC Publications

WOODWORKING

Advanced Scrollsaw Projects	GMC Publications
Beginning Picture Marquetry	Lawrence Threadgold
Bird Boxes and Feeders for the Garden	Dave Mackenzie
Celtic Carved Lovespoons: 30 Patterns	Sharon Littley & Clive Griffin
Celtic Woodcraft	Glenda Bennett
Complete Woodfinishing	Ian Hosker
David Charlesworth's Furniture-Making Techniques	David Charlesworth
David Charlesworth's Furniture-Making Techniques – Volume 2	
	David Charlesworth
The Encyclopedia of Joint Making	Terrie Noll
Furniture-Making Projects for the Wood Craftsman	GMC Publications
Furniture-Making Techniques for the Wood Craftsman	GMC Publications
Furniture Restoration (Practical Crafts)	Kevin Jan Bonner
Furniture Restoration: A Professional at Work	John Lloyd
Furniture Restoration and Repair for Beginners	Kevin Jan Bonner
Furniture Restoration Workshop	Kevin Jan Bonner
Green Woodwork	Mike Abbott
Intarsia: 30 Patterns for the Scrollsaw	John Everett
Kevin Ley's Furniture Projects	Kevin Ley
Making Chairs and Tables	GMC Publications
Making Chairs and Tables – Volume 2	GMC Publications
Making Classic English Furniture	Paul Richardson
Making Heirloom Boxes	Peter Lloyd
Making Little Boxes from Wood	John Bennett
Making Screw Threads in Wood	Fred Holder
Making Shaker Furniture	Barry Jackson
Making Woodwork Aids and Devices	Robert Wearing
Mastering the Router	Ron Fox
Pine Furniture Projects for the Home	Dave Mackenzie
Practical Scrollsaw Patterns	John Everett
Router Magic: Jigs, Fixtures and Tricks to Unleash your Router's Full Potential	Bill Hylton
Router Tips & Techniques	Robert Wearing
Routing: A Workshop Handbook	Anthony Bailey
Routing for Beginners	Anthony Bailey
Sharpening: The Complete Guide	Jim Kingshott
Sharpening Pocket Reference Book	Jim Kingshott
Simple Scrollsaw Projects	GMC Publications
Space-Saving Furniture Projects	Dave Mackenzie
Stickmaking: A Complete Course	Andrew Jones & Clive George
Stickmaking Handbook	Andrew Jones & Clive George
Storage Projects for the Router	GMC Publications
Test Reports: The Router and Furniture & Cabinetmaking	GMC Publications
Veneering: A Complete Course	Ian Hosker
Veneering Handbook	Ian Hosker
Woodfinishing Handbook (Practical Crafts)	Ian Hosker
Woodworking with the Router: Professional Router Techniques any Woodworker can Use	Bill Hylton & Fred Matlack

PHOTOGRAPHY

ART TECHNIQUES

VIDEOS

MAGAZINES

WOODTURNING ◆ WOODCARVING ◆ FURNITURE & CABINETMAKING
THE ROUTER ◆ NEW WOODWORKING ◆ THE DOLLS' HOUSE MAGAZINE
OUTDOOR PHOTOGRAPHY ◆ BLACK & WHITE PHOTOGRAPHY
MACHINE KNITTING NEWS ◆ BUSINESSMATTERS

The above represents a full list of all titles currently published or scheduled to be published.
All are available direct from the Publishers or through bookshops, newsagents and specialist retailers.
To place an order, or to obtain a complete catalogue, contact:

GMC Publications,
Castle Place, 166 High Street, Lewes, East Sussex BN7 1XU, United Kingdom
Tel: 01273 488005 Fax: 01273 478606
E-mail: pubs@thegmcgroup.com

Orders by credit card are accepted

Also by Chris & Valerie Wheeler
and available from GMC Publications

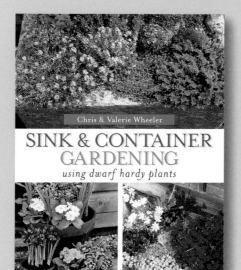

Sink & Container Gardening
using dwarf hardy plants

This book offers a wealth of planting suggestions, both traditional and innovative, together with all the practical advice you need to make your container garden a success. Six categories of plants are surveyed in detail:

dwarf shrubs and conifers • grasses and sedges • perennials • alpines • bulbs • herbs

144 pages, 276 × 210mm
107 colour photographs
10 planting plans in watercolour
5 line drawings
ISBN 1 86108 200 2

Alpine Gardening

A detailed guide to the many ways in which hardy alpines can be grown in the garden – by gardeners of all abilities, not just specialists. It covers all aspects, from choosing plants to cultivating and displaying them.

160 pages, 276 × 210mm
150 colour photographs
6 planting plans in watercolour
ISBN 1 86108 300 9